Reading, Writing, and Rhythm

Engaging Content-Area Literacy Strategies

Author
Rosalie Fink, Ed.D

SHELL EDUCATION

Publishing Credits

Corinne Burton, M.A.Ed., *President*; Conni Medina, M.A.Ed., *Managing Editor*;
Kimberly Stockton, M.Ed, *Vice President of Education*; Sara Johnson, M.S.Ed., *Content Director*;
Kristina Mazaika, M.A.Ed., *Editor*; Kyleena Harper, *Assistant Editor*; Marissa Dunham, *Editorial
Assistant*; Robin Erickson, *Multimedia Designer*; Kevin Pham, *Production Artist*

Shell Education

5301 Oceanus Drive
Huntington Beach, CA 92649-1030
http://www.shelleducation.com

ISBN 978-1-4258-0999-7

© 2015 Shell Educational Publishing, Inc.

Table of Contents

Foreword

"The longer I live, the more I see there's something about reciting rhythmical words aloud—it's almost biological—it has the ability to comfort and enliven human beings." —Robert Pinsky, *Former Poet Laureate of the United States*

One of the main reasons I believe that teaching is such a challenging task is that it is both a science and an art. The best teachers I know employ methods that are based on solid science, but they also embed in their lessons activities, language, and materials that tap in to the aesthetic side of learning.

It seems that over the past few decades, teaching—especially the teaching of reading and writing—has been viewed primarily as a science. We can go back to the work of the National Institute of Child Health and Human Development (2006) that examined scientific studies of reading development and instruction to identify scientifically valid approaches to teaching reading. These approaches have subsequently appeared in national (and state) literacy initiatives such as Reading First and the Common Core State Standards. Reading First mandated that Reading First schools employ instructional methods that were validated by "scientifically based reading research (US Department of Education 2014, para. 1)." By contrast, nothing in Reading First even hinted at the artistry of teaching reading.

Although the intent of Reading First was to have all children read at grade level by the end of third grade, the actual results were disappointing. Could it be that the disappointing results and the stagnation of reading achievement in the United States could be at least partially due to the relative exclusion of the art of teaching reading from instructional reading programs and methods?

This dearth of professional material on the art of teaching reading (and writing) is why I am so excited about Rosalie Fink's newest book *Reading, Writing, and Rhythm*. In this very practical book she provides artful and effective literacy approaches for teaching reading and writing and for employing reading and writing in the content areas. Readers will find wonderful resources such as poems, songs, raps, and more for adding that much needed aesthetic dimension to reading and writing in the various subject areas.

I might add that Dr. Fink is not new to the field of arts in literacy education. She has written extensively on this subject over many years. She has also studied successful adults who overcame early literacy difficulties. One of Dr. Fink's consistent findings was that these individuals began to flourish when they were invited into literacy in artful and aesthetic ways.

Rosalie Fink's book fills a critical need for approaching reading and writing instruction in new ways. This book fills an important gap in the literature for teachers. Reading and writing and the content areas are not only a set of discrete competencies that need to be mastered; reading and writing and the content areas can and should offer opportunities to have aesthetic experiences, to be filled with joy and wonder, and, as poet Robert Pinsky notes, to be comforted and enlivened. I wish you great joy on your journey into *Reading, Writing, and Rhythm*.

—Timothy Rasinski, Ph.D.
Kent State University

Acknowledgments

Many people helped to make this book possible. My editors at Shell Education worked tirelessly on many drafts, and I appreciate their professionalism and dedication to this project. Thanks especially to Sara Johnson, Kristina Mazaika, Kimberly Stockton, Corinne Burton, and Rachelle Cracchiolo. Thanks also to Marissa Dunham, Kyleena Harper, Dona Rice, and Robin Erickson.

Thanks to my friends and colleagues at The Harvard Graduate School of Education and Lesley University. I appreciate their deep knowledge of education and interest in my work. I'm also indebted to my students at Lesley University and many teachers and students at other schools for their interest in this book and their generous contributions of raps and poems.

I am grateful to my fabulous family: to my beloved parents, Hal and Adina Lewis, to whom I owe my lifelong excitement about teaching, reading, writing, and the arts; and to my sisters, Dorothy Putnam and Nancy Evans, and their husbands, Tom Putnam and Tedd Evans, for ongoing friendship and love and for their suggestions of poems, songs, and songbooks.

I am especially grateful to my daughters, Julia Feldman and Jennifer Fink. Their love, interest, and suggestions about the book were invaluable. They were my devoted cheerleaders and I appreciate their support. Thanks also to their spouses, Uri Feldman and Sarah Sohn, for their interest in the book and technical assistance.

I also want to thank my grandchildren: Maya, Alisa, Ben, and Nadia. I appreciate their love, youthful curiosity, and generous contributions to this book. Thanks for being an important part of my life!

Finally, thanks to my husband, Gerry, whose zest for life, love, learning, and adventure have been invaluable. I am grateful for his lifelong support of all my endeavors and his excitement about this book.

"Children love to play with rhythm and rhyme in language. This book provides a variety of activities where children from pre-school to high school can engage in word play using content. This book is a gem for teachers who want to build on concepts gained from close reading in a joyful manner!"

—Lori DiGisi, Ed.D.
ELA Department Head
Fuller Middle School, Framingham, MA
ILA Board of Directors, 2014–2017

"Rosalie Fink has done it again! The learner has once again become the center, thus leading to success all around. This time, rhythm and rhyme— key elements in literacy—have become the reason to read and the reason to write for all kinds of learners."

—Arona Gvaryahu, MA. Ed.
Israel Ministry of Education

"Rosalie Fink has written a fresh and innovative resource for educators, providing many creative ideas about facilitating literacy development through arts-based activities. Others have written about using the arts, of course, but this book emphasizes rhythm and embodied activities in a particularly insightful way. She argues convincingly that kinesthetic activities can be deeply connected to reading and writing, and she provides many practical ideas for how to bring her approach into classrooms. The book will be an invaluable resource for educators working to engage students from various backgrounds and at various levels."

—Stanton Wortham, Ph.D.
Professor of Education
University of Pennsylvania

"The future belongs to young people with an education and the imagination to create."

—President Barack Obama

Introduction

What Is This Book About?

Reading, Writing, and Rhythm is about engaging teachers in new ways to integrate literacy and content-area subjects through rhythm, the arts, and interesting experiences. The book's overarching goal is to engage diverse students, get them fired up about learning, and deepen their understanding of English language arts, science, social studies, and mathematics. The lively lessons, hands-on activities, and materials in this book are aligned with next generation standards to foster successful content-area reading and writing instruction for *all* types of students—typically developing students, English language learners, students with learning disabilities, and gifted and talented students.

Reading, Writing, and Rhythm uses the arts, students' interests, and questioning strategies to teach content-area literacy in innovative ways. The book's strategies meet goals deemed essential for developing proficiency in the following literacy skills: word recognition and reading fluency; vocabulary development; deep comprehension and close reading of complex texts; narrative, expository, and research-based reading and writing; and listening, speaking, presentation, and digital skills (Fisher and Frey 2015; Shanahan 2012; Snow 2010; National Institute of Child Health and Human Development 2000). Teacher-initiated strategies and student-centered approaches are used to guide students in becoming active creators of their own materials. The strategies in this book are designed to deepen students' content understanding and, simultaneously, foster growth and development of literacy skills at increasingly higher levels (Fink 2006; Fink and Samuels 2008; Guthrie and Alvermann 1999).

Why Use Rhythm and the Arts?

The arts have a unique capacity to promote engagement and propel learning (Bouffard 2014; Catterall, Dumais, and Hampton-Thomas 2012; Gardner 2014, 1983; Hildebrandt and Zan 2002; Hong Xu 2008; Hong Xu, Zunich, and Perkins 2007; Rasinski 2008). Most of us can recall songs, nursery rhymes, prayers, or poems that we learned as early as age 4, 5, or 6—usually before we learned to read. The reason for our poignant memories of such early multisensory learning experiences is that rhythm and rhyme have a magnetic ability to embed words and concepts indelibly in our brains. As teachers, we can take advantage of the dynamic power of art forms such as song and poetry to instill information in memory and make deep impressions. In my own teaching, I have found that you don't need experience with an art form to use it successfully. All you need is the desire to try something new. As with cooking a new recipe, if you follow instructions, you can get great results.

One of the most compelling reasons for teaching with the arts is that the arts increase student engagement and are associated with improved academic achievement (Bouffard 2014). Recently, educators have noted that some students involved in arts-rich experiences achieve higher scores on report cards and standardized tests across content subjects, regardless of whether the art form is drawing, painting, poetry, rap, music, dance, or drama (Bouffard 2014; Donovan and Pascale 2012; Gibas 2012; Yenawine 2013).

For many years, Howard Gardner has emphasized the importance of the arts and multisensory approaches to education based on his theory of multiple intelligences. Recently, he explicitly urged educators to teach important concepts and ideas pluralistically in his keynote lecture at The Excellence in Special Education Summit (2014). By "teaching pluralistically," Gardner meant teaching through multisensory modalities by using the arts. Gardner's reason was clear and straightforward: If you teach pluralistically, using all of the senses and the arts whenever possible, then you reach more students. What could be more important than that?

Reading, Writing, and Rhythm reaches out to more students from diverse backgrounds by showing teachers how to tap into students' familiarity with rap, song, poetry, and other engaging art forms to connect to content-area concepts and literacy skills. The book presents highly engaging materials created by classroom teachers and their students. The materials and activities can be used in a wide variety of classroom settings. *Reading, Writing, and Rhythm* provides fresh new protocols with easy-to-follow instructions to help teachers guide students to create their own raps, songs, reader's theater scripts, discussion questions, and more. Each activity is designed to promote engagement, enhance content mastery, develop literacy skills, and meet the goals of today's rigorous standards.

How Is The Book Organized?

The activities and materials in *Reading, Writing, and Rhythm* are designated for students in grades K–2, 3–5, and the secondary grades. Each chapter provides a pre-reading anticipation guide and a post-reading reflection and discussion guide to encourage thought-provoking discussions among educators. These discussions can be conducted in a variety of ways, such as pairs, grade-level teams, professional learning communities, or book study groups. Each chapter of the book supplies engaging examples of content-specific vocabulary activities, discussion questions, raps, poems, Reader's Theater scripts, and other activities that are effective for teaching content in many subjects. The book also encourages students to create their own original content-specific rap songs, reader's theater scripts, body movements, and discussion questions.

Chapter 1 presents an Interest-Based Model of Content-Area Literacy and the Arts. The model uses students' passionate personal interests and the arts as centerpieces of instruction. Activities in Chapter 1 enable teachers to use students' personal interests and the arts to motivate and engage them in learning. The chapter is based on my study of individuals whose success in literacy and in life was spurred by a passionate personal interest. Each individual's personal interests provided the impetus for deep learning in reading, writing, and content-area knowledge. For many of the individuals, arts-based learning inspired their success.

Chapter 1 also presents a framework for teaching in all the content areas. It includes specific protocols for teaching through students' individual interests, students' questions, and various art forms. The chapter introduces strategies and easy-to-follow, step-by-step protocols for creating original rap songs, Reader's Theater scripts, poems, and movement sequences. Each of these strategies has been used successfully and effectively across grade levels.

Chapters 2–5 focus separately on the different content areas and show teachers how to meet today's standards in English language arts, science, social studies, and mathematics. These chapters apply the strategies and protocols presented in Chapter 1 to specific content-area material. For example, they demonstrate specific ways for teachers and students to create raps, poems, and Reader's Theater scripts to master new vocabulary, facts, and concepts.

Chapter 2 presents strategies and materials for teaching English language arts. **Chapter 3** focuses on strategies and materials for teaching science. **Chapter 4** presents strategies and materials for promoting inquiry and mastery of social studies and historical concepts. Finally, **Chapter 5** presents strategies and materials for teaching mathematics.

Reading, Writing, and Rhythm promotes important 21st century educational goals that aim to:

- Tap into students' curiosity and get them excited about reading and writing in all content areas

- Improve students' content-area vocabulary and conceptual knowledge

- Enhance students' questioning ability and critical thinking

- Develop students' confidence in taking tests and raise their test scores

- Prepare students to be ready for college, careers, and active civic participation (Lander 2015)

- "Excite kids with significant ideas and issues that permeate today's world—and then give them the strategies they need" to succeed (Harvey 2015, 31).

My Hopes for Readers

I have used many of the strategies and materials in this book successfully with my own students. I hope that readers are inspired, as I was, by students' excitement as they become fully engaged in intriguing activities that provide new ways of learning. I hope that the approaches in this book enable teachers to help all types of students become curious questioners, deep thinkers, and enthusiastic readers and writers. My goal is to help diverse students develop higher-level literacy skills and content knowledge through the activities provided here—activities that can simultaneously engage, delight, and instruct our students. I am interested in hearing how other teachers use the activities in this book and can be reached at rfink@lesley.edu. Good luck with your students!

—Rosalie Fink
www.rosaliefink.com

Chapter 1

A Foundation for Reading, Writing, and Rhythm in the Classroom

Questions to Activate Thinking

1. How do you currently use your students' interests, curiosity, and the arts to support learning?

2. What do you hope to learn from this chapter about integrating students' interests, questions, and the arts into your lessons?

3. How do you think this chapter could help your students meet state or national standards?

Using Students' Interests

Teachers intuitively know that students come to school with outside interests that can be harnessed for learning. Recently, researchers have studied the power of students' out-of-school interests to improve learning in school (Fink 2008, 2006; Guthrie, Klauda, and Ho 2013; Hartman 1997; Hong Xu, Zunich, and Perkins 2007). More than ever before, teachers today are tapping into students' interests in sports, superheroes, nature, music, dance, gymnastics, and gaming. Our increasing awareness of the positive role of students' interests arose from teachers' experiences in real classrooms, including my own experiences teaching in a public school in New York (Fink forthcoming 2016, 2008, 2006; Fischer and Fusaro, 2008; Guthrie, Klauda, and Ho 2013; Harvey 2015; Renninger and Hidi forthcoming).

One year I noticed five bright, enthusiastic students in my English language arts class. They consistently sparked class discussions with their creative ideas, yet something about them perplexed me. There seemed to be a deep gulf between their complex ideas about literature on the one hand, and their lack of basic reading skills on the other hand. I wondered, "What's going on?" I had come across Eileen Simpson's book *Reversals* (1979), which included intriguing vignettes about Simpson's experiences as a girl with dyslexia. Moved by Simpson's story, I thought it might be relevant to my students, so I read an excerpt aloud to my class.

A few days later, I received notes from several mothers, thanking me for reading *Reversals* to the class, each one telling me how much it had helped her child learn that other smart people had struggled with reading and writing, yet ultimately succeeded. The powerful impact of Simpson's story sparked my curiosity about others who had struggled with reading yet ultimately succeeded. I wanted to learn more about them and find out what led to their success, both as readers and as professionals.

So I conducted a study with a group of individuals from all over the United States who had struggled with reading, yet eventually succeeded in fields that required lots of reading and writing—fields such as medicine, law, business, theater, art, psychology, education, biology, and physics. Many of these individuals were outstanding professionals who were major movers and shakers in their fields. I traveled around the country administering literacy and psychological tests and assessments to them and conducted lengthy face-to-face interviews with each person. As I listened to their fascinating life stories, I was struck by the depths of their academic struggles, as well as the heights of their ultimate successes.

Ronald W. Davis' Story

I interviewed Dr. Ronald W. Davis, one of the greatest living innovators of the 21st century (Allan 2013). Dr. Davis is Professor of Biochemistry and Genetics and Director of the Stanford University Genome Technology Center. His groundbreaking scientific research is responsible for many of the major genetic advances of the past 20 years (Allan 2013). Davis has won numerous prestigious awards, such as The Gruber Prize in Genetics in 2011, and The Warren Alpert Foundation Prize in 2013. In view of his remarkable accomplishments, I was surprised when Dr. Davis told me he had failed classes and was left back in school due to his reading difficulties. He vividly recalled his painful struggles learning to read and write.

"I was at the bottom in reading skills and spelling skills. I was a very, very slow reader and couldn't read out loud or silently. It began in first grade and continued in second grade, third grade, fourth grade, and on and on and on..." (Fink 2006, 71)

I had expected to learn that Dr. Davis had conducted scientific experiments without really reading much. However, as I listened to him, I realized that, on the contrary, he was actually an avid reader who loved reading science materials, beginning at an early age. As a boy, Davis was an avid young reader propelled by his passionate personal interest—science.

"You read science for how things are put together. My interest in chemistry...started with my interest in airplanes in grade school... that quickly converted to propellant systems in 7th and 8th grades." (Fink 2006, 71)

Dr. Davis was motivated by an intense interest in science and what Professor Ellen Winner of Boston College calls "a rage to master" a subject (1996). Despite his severe dyslexia and difficulties with basic, lower level visual and phonological reading skills, he engaged in close reading of advanced science books—complex texts apparently well above the reading level of his peers. The type of close reading of complex texts that Dr. Davis engaged in is a compelling goal of the Common Core and other state standards.

"When I was a freshman in high school, I read quite a few college texts. I became fascinated with nitrogen chemistry, so I got organic chemistry textbooks from my teacher." (Fink 2006, 71)

Dr. Davis, like the individuals in my study, was spurred by intense curiosity about a topic of passionate personal interest. Each of them read voraciously, engaging in what Jeanne Chall called "reading to learn" (1996). Propelled by their intellectual curiosity to learn more, they described their own passions for "reading to learn" about a topic of passionate personal interest:

> *"I did a lot of reading. I loved reading about physics, so I got lots of physics magazines and books, and I just read about physics on my own."*
> —James Bensinger, physicist (Fink 2006, 8; 2008, 1998)

> *"I remember reading many, many historical novels, particularly about the Tudor and Stuart periods. Because mainly they were lovely love stories!"* (Fink 2006, 95)
> –Ann L. Brown, educational researcher

> *"I loved history.... I'm a Civil War buff, mainly 'cause I like Lincoln. So through reading about Lincoln, I've learned lots of other things— including learning how to read!"* (Fink 2006, 8)
> —C. Ellen Corduan, theater set designer/ teacher

By reading extensively about a topic they found personally fascinating, each individual in my study developed deep knowledge of the schema of a favorite content area; this included learning its specific vocabulary, themes, questions, concepts, and typical text structures. Based on their schema familiarity, they used the context effectively to make smart guesses and learn new words and concepts. Their intense and repeated reading about a single favorite topic enhanced their depth of background knowledge and, simultaneously, enabled them to gain lots of reading practice. The repetition and redundant text material itself provided some of the requisite drill and practice they needed to develop reading fluency and deep understanding (Fink 2006, 2008; Rasinski and Samuels 2011).

Their topics of personal interest varied. Figure 1.1 summarizes their favorite topics and genres.

Figure 1.1 Favorite Content Areas/Genres

Women		Men	
Favorite Content Area/ Genre	Number of Responses	Favorite Content Area/ Genre	Number of Responses
novels	23	novels	14
biographies	2	biographies	2
science	2	science	5
social studies	1	social studies	6
cooking	1	auto shop	1
no data	1	sailing	1
		poetry	1
total	30	total	30

Gender differences in topics of high-interest reading were statistically significant, suggesting that the differences were not due to chance alone (chi square = 5.71, p = .017).

An Interest-Based Model of Content-Area Literacy

Results from the interviews and tests led to an Interest-Based Model of Content-Area Literacy that I developed (Fink 2012, 2008, 2006, 1996; Fink, Wauhkonen, and Pluto 2012). This model places student interest at the center of teaching and learning and relies on teachers as marvelous mentors who open the door to student success. The model involves tapping into students' individual interests and providing reading materials and writing activities based on their interests.

Teachers provide a key to success in The Interest-Based Model of Content-Area Literacy. They can be marvelous mentors who encourage each student and provide compelling materials about students' interests. The Interest-Based Model has seven components, as shown in Figure 1.2. Suggestions for implementing components of the model are described in Chapters 2–5.

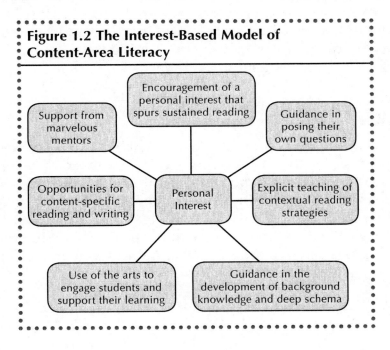

Figure 1.2 The Interest-Based Model of Content-Area Literacy

- Encouragement of a personal interest that spurs sustained reading
- Support from marvelous mentors
- Guidance in posing their own questions
- Opportunities for content-specific reading and writing
- Personal Interest
- Explicit teaching of contextual reading strategies
- Use of the arts to engage students and support their learning
- Guidance in the development of background knowledge and deep schema

Intentional Planning

The first three components of the model entail intentional planning on the part of the teacher in order to capitalize on each student's interests. First, the teacher explicitly encourages each student to pursue a personal interest, spurring motivation for sustained reading. In addition to encouraging students' interests, the teacher plans regular opportunities for students to engage in content-specific reading and writing about their topics. For example, the teacher may plan a regular Sustained Silent Reading (SSR) period at the same time each day. While students are reading, the teacher circulates to guide each student's development of background knowledge and deep schema about the topic, asking questions and planning discussions about students' topics. This questioning and ongoing discussion helps students build background knowledge and, ultimately, develop deep schema about their topics. Moreover, the teacher also guides students individually to locate additional books and websites on their topics, thus promoting extensive reading. This kind of extensive, sustained reading about a topic helps students develop the necessary background information and deep schema that lead to deep understanding of complex texts—a goal of the Common Core and other state standards.

Using Context

The teacher also provides explicit instruction in effective strategies for using the context to promote comprehension. This means calling students' attention to the surrounding words and ideas within a text in order to guide them to make "smart guesses" and predictions about the text's meanings. Learning specific ways to use the context enhances textual understanding and promotes reading proficiency at increasingly higher levels.

The individuals in my study ultimately developed the highest levels of proficient literacy—regardless of whether their favorite topic was physics, chemistry, Civil War history, architecture, etc. They scored high on all objective tests and assessments in vocabulary knowledge and reading comprehension. By reading avidly about a topic of personal interest, they developed schema familiarity and background knowledge that supported their development of high-level literacy.

When confronted with new, unfamiliar words, they used a strategy of contextual guessing based on the context. Their contextual guessing was more likely to be correct based on their schema familiarity and deep background knowledge.

> "*I used context a lot to guess at new words.*"
> —Barbara Bikofsky, special educator (Fink 1998, 324)

> "*I tended to be, you know, fairly context-driven. So I made assumptions very quickly based on context and usually substituted a reasonable word.*"
>
> —Alexander Goldowsky, museum coordinator (Fink 2002, 122)

> "*Even today, when I can't figure out a word, I guess from the context. I guess what makes sense and usually have it right.*"
> —Baruj Benacerraf, Nobel Prize winning immunologist (Fink 2006, 12; Fink and Samuels 2008)

Developing Questions

The individuals in my study asked their own questions and embarked on finding their own answers. Motivated by intellectual curiosity about their favorite topics, they sought answers to questions from reading and hands-on activities.

> *"I set up a lab in my basement and did experiments with compounds that I got from chemical supply companies.... That early experience was useful— asking your own questions, doing your own experiments, and building your own confidence by doing these things."*
> —Ronald W. Davis, genomic scientist (Fink 2006, 72; 2003)

Learning Through the Arts

The arts are powerful venues for teaching in a variety of content areas. Increasingly, educators today attest to the power of the arts to enliven lessons and engage all types of students (Bouffard 2014; Donovan and Pascale 2012; Fiske 1999; Gardner 2014; Gibas 2012). Harvard psychologist Howard Gardner frames the arts as a way to motivate learning and teach discipline. According to Gardner, art is inextricably linked to human development and woefully excluded from the school curriculum (2014, 1983).

Many of the individuals in my study learned through a variety of art forms. For example, Ann Brown, an educational researcher, loved to dance and, as a young girl, excelled as a dancer. Although she didn't learn to read fluently until age 13, the fact that she excelled in dance gave her an outlet for personal expression and joy. Perhaps most importantly, excelling in dance enabled Ann Brown to be a star and develop confidence in her own abilities.

"*I was very, very successful as a dancer; I won medals for my dancing! Dancing was a great outlet that provided joy in my life; excelling in dance gave me the confidence that I could succeed in things if I worked hard.*"
—Ann L. Brown, educational researcher (personal interview with Ann L. Brown, 1996)

Ultimately, Ann Brown became a famous educational researcher and professor at the University of California at Berkeley. She earned many prestigious awards for her outstanding contributions to the field of metacognition and literacy research. Professor Brown's influential research is cited widely today and used by teachers all over the world. The art of dance played an important role in Ann Brown's ultimate success by building her self-confidence in her abilities.

Marvelous Mentors

Each individual in my study specifically recalled marvelous mentors who helped them succeed despite their difficulties. They were especially grateful to these memorable teachers, who made a huge difference in their lives. They remember them with reverence and gratitude.

"*Mr. Tilman is a teacher I'll never forget. He got me psyched about reading by using comics and art, which fascinated me!*"
—Cruz Sanabria, early childhood educator (Fink 2006, 47)

"*In fifth grade, I finally learned to read; it was a big change! I remember it clearly: My teacher, Mrs. King, helped me. I owe it all to Mrs. King!*"
—James Bensinger, physicist (Fink 2006, 2003)

> *"My high school biology teacher encouraged me to read more science books and take more science courses. He helped me with my experiments on plants and put me in contact with a biology professor at Eastern Illinois University."*
> —Ronald W. Davis, genomics scientist (Fink 2006, 72)

Discovering Students' Interests

Teachers played pivotal roles in nurturing the personal interests of these individuals and promoting their success. Similarly, teachers today can determine what interests each student has and nurture those interests. Teachers can discover each student's interests by using one of the many Reading Interest Inventories available, such as the one in Figure 1.3. Another strategy is to use an autobiographical Bio Poem or I-Poem, shown in Figures 1.4 and 1.5. Each of these activities will help familiarize teachers with their own students' interests.

Reading Interest Inventories

Reading Interest Inventories (RIIs) are short surveys that reveal a student's favorite topics and genres; they provide a wonderful way for teachers to ascertain what topics excite each student. In my own classes, I have found the Sample Reading Interest Inventory in Figure 1.3 to be especially helpful at the beginning of each school year; however, it can be used at any time when a teacher wants to learn more about a student. Reading Interest Inventories provide a great way for students and teachers to get to know each other in a comfortable, low-key setting. The teacher can informally administer an RII orally to a student, while other students work quietly. Older students can fill out the written Reading Interest Inventory individually and then hand it to the teacher.

Reading Interest Inventories are also an effective way to address the important speaking and listening goals of the Common Core State Standards. This is especially the case when students work in pairs and interview each other, which can be done easily with students in grades 3 or 4 and up. The student interviewer asks questions aloud, the interviewee replies, and finally, the interviewer records the interviewee's responses in writing. This activity is fun and provides a good way for students to bond and get to know each other, while the teacher learns more about each individual's interests. Moreover, since Reading Interest Inventories have no right or wrong answers, they create a relaxed social learning environment while revealing lots of important information about each student in a relatively short amount of time.

After administering the Reading Interest Inventory, teachers can use the results to select reading materials based on each student's interests. For students who have not had opportunities to discover or develop interests, I suggest using clues from the student's favorite media subjects to discover their dormant, underlying interests. The sample Reading Interest Inventory in Figure 1.3 can be used across grade levels.

Figure 1.3 Sample Reading Interest Inventory

- What are some books that were read to you?
- What are some books that you have read yourself?
- What are some of your hobbies?
- What after-school activities do you like?
- What are some movies that you like?
- What television shows do you watch?
- What are some computer games, websites, or apps that you like?
- What school subjects interest you?
- What pets, sports, or art activities do you like?
- If you could take a trip, where would you go? Why would you like to go there?
- What jobs or careers interest you? Why?

(Adapted from Roe, Smith, and Burns 2011; Fink 2006; Fink and Samuels 2008)

Teachers can also modify the Reading Interest Inventory to suit their own students' needs and administer it in various ways. The following are adaptations for various grade ranges.

Reading Interest Inventory Ideas

Grades K–2

The teacher orally asks questions from the Reading Interest Inventory. Then, the teacher records the students' responses.

Grades 3–5

Depending on the needs and levels of the class, students either respond to the inventory questions in writing, or the teacher writes the students' responses.

Secondary

Students write their own responses to questions on the Reading Interest Inventory. Or, students ask a partner the inventory questions and write down their partner's responses.

Bio Poems and I-Poems

Another quick, effective way to learn about a student's interests is to use Bio Poems and I-Poems. (See Figures 1.4 and 1.5.) These easy-to-use templates encourage students to write and draw pictures about themselves. The Bio Poem template is useful for students across ages and grade levels. Bio Poems and I-Poems are easy to modify and adapt to suit the ages and developmental stages of different groups of students.

Figure 1.4 Sample Bio Poem

Line 1: First name only

Line 2: Four traits that describe you

Line 3: Siblings of _____ (or son/daughter of _____)

Line 4: Loves _____, _____, _____ (3 people or things)

Line 5: Who feels _____, _____, _____ (3 items)

Line 6: Who needs _____, _____, _____ (3 items)

Line 7: Who gives _____, _____, _____ (3 items)

Line 8: Who fears _____, _____, _____ (3 items)

Line 9: Who would like to see _____, _____, _____ (3 items)

Line 10: Resident of (your street), (your city)

Line 11: Your last name (draw a picture of yourself)

(Adapted by Minnie Gross, Florida middle school teacher)

Figure 1.5 Sample I-Poem

I am _____
I wonder _____
I hear _____
I see _____
I want _____
I am _____
I pretend _____
I feel _____
I touch _____
I worry _____
I cry _____
I am _____
I understand _____
I say _____
I dream _____

(Reprinted from Kucan 2007)

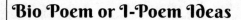

Bio Poem or I-Poem Ideas

Grades K–2

The teacher reads the questions aloud and writes the students' responses.

Grades 3–5

Students write their own responses and then share them aloud with a partner, a small group, or the whole class.

Secondary

Each student writes down a partner's responses. Afterwards, students share their responses with a different partner or a small group.

Resources to Support Students' Interests

After discovering what intrigues a student, busy teachers face the challenge of finding books and websites to match each student's interests. The following resources provide lists of highly recommended books and websites on specific topics. These lists make library trips more purposeful and productive but, of course, don't preclude the fun of browsing.

Book Lists to Support Students' Interests

- *100 Best Books for Children* (Silvey 2004)—This is an outstanding resource for matching students to books of interest. It includes a concise plot summary and age range for each title.

- *A to Zoo: Subject Access to Students' Picture Books* (Lima and Lima 2006)—This resource is excellent for finding books on the interests of young children. It lists preschool and elementary books alphabetically by topic.

- *Bookmatch: How to Scaffold Student Book Selection for Independent Reading* (Wedwick and Wutz 2008)—The Bookmatch system helps each child self-select a book, rate it according to specific criteria, and make an independent decision about a book choice. This system is based on criteria including readability level, book length, language, organization, prior knowledge of the topic, genre appeal, text manageability, topic appropriateness, connections to another book or life experience, and high (or low) interest of the book to the student. Bookmatch provides websites with additional resources, reproducible charts, and specific criteria to help primary and intermediate students self-select "just right" books independently.

- *Bright Beginnings for Boys: Engaging Young Boys in Active Literacy* (Zambo and Brozo 2009)—This excellent book for teachers presents book suggestions as well as new ways to approach literacy teaching for boys in primary and intermediate grades.

- *Great Books for Boys: More Than 600 Books for Boys 2–14* (Odean 1997)—This annotated list has fascinating books that will interest many boys. The author's goal is to avoid gender stereotypes while recommending books likely to appeal to boys with a wide range of interests and personalities.

- *Great Books for Girls: More Than 600 Books to Inspire Today's Girls and Tomorrow's Women* (Odean 1997)—This unique annotated book list contains stories with heroines who are active, creative, articulate, and intelligent. Girls in these books meet difficult challenges, resolve conflicts, and engage in adventures and active quests and experiences.

Teaching with Rhythm and Rap

Rhythm, rhyme, and rap are powerful hooks that spark students' interests and engage them in learning. There are many creative ways to use these art forms to support instruction and deepen learning in all the content areas.

In their compelling book, *Hip-Hop Poetry and the Classics,* Alan Sitomer and Michael Cirelli (2004) argue convincingly that rap lyrics possess the same literary components as classical poems and can be used effectively to teach poetry. Sitomer and Cirelli explain that rap lyrics and traditional poems share the following key literary elements: alliteration, allusion, figurative language, imagery, irony, metaphor, simile, onomatopoeia, rhyme schemes, mood, theme, meaning, and so forth. For example, Sitomer and Cirelli demonstrate how the classic poem "Harlem: A Dream Deferred" by Langston Hughes (1958) and the rap "Juicy" by Notorious B.I.G. (1994) both use powerful imagery and share universal themes. In these two pieces, reaching for your dreams is a shared universal theme. In addition to encouraging students to strive for high goals, lofty ambitions, and personal dreams, both of these literary works explore the devastating outcomes that can result when individuals ignore their own dreams for too long—sadness, stress, inner decay, anger, and self-destruction, to name a few. (Note: "Juicy" includes explicit lyrics and strong content. Please review the lyrics closely to determine whether they are appropriate to use with students, and consider blacking out offensive content. It is not recommended for students younger than high school.)

In keeping with suggestions for instruction in Sitomer and Cirelli's captivating book, teachers can use their own students' fascination with pop culture as a way to draw in *all* types of students and help them appreciate classic poetry as well as rap. By demonstrating literary elements that the two genres share, teachers entice and empower students to recognize the relevance and power of rap as well as classics of the literary canon.

In my own teaching, I have discovered that rap is a great way to meet the goals of state and national standards. One activity that has proven very successful is guiding students to write their own raps based on themes or favorite excerpts or vignettes from a text. This activity inspired my students' enthusiasm and enhanced their ability to read complex texts closely, develop analytical comprehension skills, review content in great detail, and relate a text in a meaningful way to their own lives.

By integrating rap into the regular curriculum, teachers can use students' out-of-school interests as assets to learning academic subjects *in school*. Rap can be used to teach new material as well as to reinforce what students have previously learned. Perhaps most importantly, I have found that when students invent a new rap themselves, they experience the excitement and joy of creation and an authentic sense of accomplishment and pride. What's more, their self-confidence soars!

Create a Rap

One way for teachers to use rap and other art forms is by following step-by-step protocols, such as The Rap Protocol. I have used The Rap Protocol successfully in my own classes and have worked with many teachers who find the steps fun to do and easy to follow. The Rap Protocol can be easily adapted for any content area or grade level.

The gradual release of responsibility model has teachers slowly and gradually relinquish responsibility from themselves to their students.

The Rap Protocol can be used for a whole class, pairs of students, or small groups—especially when teachers use a gradual release of responsibility approach. As students work in pairs or small groups, they learn the step-by-step sequence of The Rap Protocol and become increasingly independent as rap artists. In the process of creating raps, students discuss and master challenging content-area facts and concepts. The concepts and vocabulary of their raps depend on the topic or content area they are studying. Topics of student raps can range from simple routines, such as learning clean-up time routines, to complex science material, such as learning the process of photosynthesis or the scientific method. In my own classes, I have found that all types of raps work well—published raps, teacher-made raps, and student-created raps.

Using The Rap Protocol

After students read an assigned (or self-selected) chapter or book, the teacher can introduce rap as a genre for reviewing and deepening their understanding. The teacher can explain how rap's use of literary elements such as alliteration, allusion, rhythm, and rhyme is similar to the use of the same literary elements in classic poems by Tennyson, Keats, Frost, Whitman, or Shakespeare. Then, the teacher can select one or two literary elements as a focus for each lesson, depending on the needs of the class.

To begin, the teacher models by reading a rap aloud, such as "The MCAS Rap," a rap from the appendix of this book, or a rap found on the Internet. Then, the teacher guides students as they follow The Rap Protocol (Figure 1.6), which is designed to help students of all ages create their own original raps about the content they are learning.

Figure 1.6 The Rap Protocol

1. The teacher tells students to use rhythm and rhyme to create a rap about their chapter or book, explaining that not every line must rhyme. (In addition, the teacher can also encourage students to use alliteration and rhymes within a line.)

2. The teacher explains that students' raps should use language appropriate for performing in school.

3. After writing their rap, students practice reading it aloud expressively and rhythmically, adding gestures, clapping, body movement, or costumes.

4. Students then perform their rap for the class. An additional option is to record the performances and then post them on a classroom website or blog. Students can also perform their raps live for families, school assemblies, or nursing homes.

5. Students display their written raps on bulletin boards in the classroom or school display cases. They can also publish their work in school newsletters or online student newspapers. (Note: Accompanying art work can also be encouraged and displayed.)

Using Student- and Teacher-Created Raps

Student-created raps are a great way for students to consolidate what they've learned. They can be used to review for weekly quizzes, midterms, or other tests and assessments. Raps are also a good way to help students review material to help them meet state and national goals and standards.

In the rap that follows, each student in a third–grade inner-city class in Boston, Massachusetts, created a line in the rap to review good test-taking techniques. This helped them prepare for the state-mandated MCAS test (Massachusetts Comprehensive Assessment System). Creating and chanting "The MCAS Rap" not only helped these third-graders improve their test-taking skills, but also increased their self-confidence. Other sample raps included here are "The First Day Rap" and the "Clean-Up Time Rap." See Appendix B for additional songs, raps, and poems.

The MCAS Rap
Pseudonyms are used in place of students' real names.

Chorus

We are here today
To rap about a test
Called the MCAS
So you can do your best.

Verse 1

My name is Kenisha and the first thing that you do
Is to read the directions all the way through.
My name is TJ, and the next step that you take
Is to read the title; don't take a break.
My name is Savari, and the next thing that you do
Is to read the italics; that is what you do.
My name is Erin, and the fourth thing that you do
Is to read the questions, then go back and review.

Chorus

Verse 2

My name is Bill, and after we review,
You start the story; that is what you do.
My name is Chris, and when we find the answer
We make sure to highlight to get the right answer.
My name is Deidre, and I have a suggestion
After you highlight, read the next question.
My name is Maya, and we've shown you the way
To conquer the MCAS, so have a nice day!

This rap is about students' excitement on the first day of school. It's a great conversation starter and a nice way to introduce the school year.

First Day Rap

by Dona Herweck Rice

Look out world,
Here I come,
Ready to learn and have some fun!

Shoes on my feet,
Thoughts in my head,
Pencil's been sharpened and my tummy's been fed.

Desks are ready,
Shiny and clean.
For the most curious kids ever seen.

Teacher at the doors,
Saying hello,
Students lined up, ready to go.

It's a brand new day,
It's a brand new year!
Come on, class, it's time to cheer!

Hip hip hoorah!
Hip hip hooray!
A brand new school year starts today!

This rap was written for teaching classroom routines in grades K–2. It helps give students a heads up about what to expect. Chanting this rap is fun and provides an excellent way to help young students make a smooth transition from one activity to the next. (Note: this is meant as a "call and response" rap. Teacher says, "Ringa-ding-ding! Hear the chime?" and kids respond, "Clean-up time! Clean-up time!" Then teacher asks, "Dirty floor?" and kids answer, "Not any more," and so on.)

Clean-Up Time Rap

by Dona Herweck Rice

Ringa-ding-ding!

Hear the chime?
    Clean-up time!
    Clean-up time!
Dirty floor?
    Not anymore!
Messy desks?
    We won't rest!
Books off rack?
    Put them back!
Toys askew?
    That won't do!
Come on team!
    Let's get clean!

Comparing Rap and Traditional Poetry

Rap and traditional poetry are similar in many ways because they both include many of the same literary features: alliteration, allusion, figurative language, hyperbole, imagery, irony, theme, metaphor, simile, mood creation, onomatopoeia, personification, symbolism, rhythm patterns, rhyme schemes, and so forth. Most raps today are intended to accompany dancing; consequently, rap's distinctive rhythms and beats are typically strong and powerful. However, this is not necessarily the case with classic poetry; the rhythms of classic poems follow patterns that may be subtle compared to the signature rhythms of rap. Rap is written in iambic pentameter, which gives rap music the sensation of being behind the beat. Moreover, the content and ideas of rap and classic poetry typically differ—but not always.

Reflect and Discuss

1. What are some possible benefits of using students' interests as part of literacy and content-area lessons?

2. Which of the protocols, strategies, and materials in this chapter would you like to use in an upcoming lesson? What do you need to do to plan for this?

3. What challenges might you encounter using these protocols, strategies, or materials, and how could you handle them?

Chapter 2

Reading, Writing, and Rhythm in English Language Arts

Questions to Activate Thinking

1. What aspects of teaching English language arts do you find most rewarding and meaningful? Why?

2. What aspects of teaching English language arts do you find most challenging? Why?

3. What types of strategies and materials do you currently use in your English language arts instruction?

4. What ideas do you have already for how to use rhythm in English language arts instruction?

English language arts provides the foundation of learning in all content subjects (Allington 2009; Snow, Burns, and Griffin 1998; Werner and Smith 1992). Consequently, a teacher's approach to motivating students and teaching them English can affect how they approach learning in all the content areas. Recent research from cognitive science, neuroscience, psychology, and education suggests that multisensory approaches that actively engage all of the student's senses can help reach and teach all types of students (Sousa 2010, 2011). The goal of this chapter is to present engaging, multisensory activities and materials that enable all types of students to succeed and simultaneously meet state and national standards in English language arts.

The National Institute of Child Health and Human Development recommends a balanced approach to teaching English at all grade levels (Shanahan 2006). This means including basic skills, such as phonemic awareness, phonics, and word identification, as well as higher-level skills, such as vocabulary knowledge, factual and inferential comprehension, creative writing, and research skills. A balanced approach to teaching English also means using meaningful texts in a variety of genres as early as pre-K and kindergarten and all the way through the higher grades.

Teaching Phonics and Phonemic Awareness

We know that speech and language develop naturally without direct instruction; most children learn to speak naturally by listening to those around them (Wolf 2008). In contrast, learning phonemic awareness and phonics skills does not come naturally (Chall 1996; Wolf 2008). Learning phonemic awareness and phonics requires a teacher's direct, systematic instruction about the relationship between speech sounds and letters or letter groups (Chall 1996; Wolf 2008).

Phonemic awareness—the understanding that speech consists of groups of individual sounds—is an early literacy skill that helps develop decoding, word recognition, and spelling ability. Phonics, or phonological decoding, requires the knowledge that letters and groups of letters correspond to specific sounds.

Fortunately, many effective strategies that incorporate rhythm are available for teaching young children phonemic awareness, the alphabet, and the sound-symbol relationships of letters. The following list contains several suggestions for teaching these skills.

- Teach "The Alphabet Song," and have students sing it often. "The Alphabet Song" is fun and gives students a framework to use in learning to read and spell. Later, they can use their knowledge of the alphabet as a reference when learning dictionary skills.

- Teach the sounds of the letters, focusing early on letters with special meaning to students. For example, in the early grades, begin with the first letter of each child's name so that letters have personal meaning.

- Read poems or stories aloud that have rhymes embedded in them in order to help students develop phonemic awareness.

- Read alphabet books regularly with young children and make alphabet books readily available for them to browse and read.

Great Alphabet Books

- *A Is for Musk Ox* by Erin Cabatingan and Matthew Myers—Musk Ox is rambunctious and claims that A is for Musk Ox because he is Awesome and lives in Alaska, which is in the Arctic!

- *Alphabet Trucks* by Samantha R. Vamos—This informational alphabet book uses work trucks from A to Z and explains what each truck does.

- *Curious George's ABCs* by H. A. Rey—This humorous alphabet book is beautifully illustrated and has become a well-loved classic.

- *Z Is for Moose* by Kelly Bingham—This funny, award-winning alphabet book charts the shenanigans of a zebra and a moose through the alphabet.

An effective way to promote phonemic awareness is for teachers to provide lots of rich experiences with rhyming. Narratives and poems of all kinds can be used. One example is *Elmo's Rockin' Rhyme Time!* by Naomi Kleinberg (2012). This lively poetry narrative is great for teaching rhyming to young children. While the teacher reads the book aloud, children can clap, stomp their feet, bang drums, click sticks together, play triangles, or supply an ending word to complete the rhyme.

Another book that promotes phonemic awareness is *Whiny Whiny Rhino* by Carmin Iadonisi and Amanda Word (2015). This rhyming book is about a rhinoceros who is the youngest child in the family. He has many fears, both social and physical, yet, through numerous hilarious adventures, he overcomes each fear one at a time—all through catchy, unforgettable rhymes.

In addition, *Hop Like a Bunny! Waddle Like a Duck!* by Melinda Rakoncay (1987) also contains fabulous lively rhymes that are superb for building phonemic awareness. Have children chant, move, and act out the motions of each animal to enhance lessons with multisensory learning while reading this book. For example, students can:

- do the Penguin Polka;
- crawl on their bellies like inchworms; and
- bang their chests, stamp their feet, and "swing their arms to the jungle beat" like gorillas (Rakoncay 1987, 3).

Moving to rhymes with their bodies helps young children develop phonemic awareness in a fun, engaging, multisensory way that simultaneously taps their visual, auditory, and kinesthetic senses.

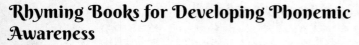

Rhyming Books for Developing Phonemic Awareness

- *A Child's Anthology of Poetry* edited by Elizabeth Hauge Sword
- *A Lot of Otters* by Barbara Helen Berger
- *Animal Crackers: Nursery Rhymes* by Jane Dyer
- *Barnyard Dance!* by Sandra Boynton
- *Crazy Hair* by Neil Gaiman
- *Green Eggs and Ham* by Dr. Seuss
- *Is Your Mama a Llama?* by Deborah Guarino
- *Jamberry* by Bruce Degen
- *Pish, Posh, Said Hieronymus Bosch* by Nancy Willard
- *Quiet Loud* by Leslie Patricelli
- *Rosie Revere, Engineer* by Andrea Beaty
- *Talking to the Sun: An Illustrated Anthology of Poems for Young People* edited by Kenneth Koch and Kate Farrell
- *Ten Little Rabbits* by Virginia Grossman and Sylvia Long
- *The Cat in the Hat* by Dr. Seuss
- *The Cat in the Hat Comes Back* by Dr. Seuss
- *The Jolly Postman* by Janet and Allan Ahlberg

Using Games and Activities for Phonemic Awareness and Phonics

Word games are another effective way to teach phonemic awareness and teach what Jeanne Chall called "the alphabetic principle"—the concept that letters and letter combinations correspond to specific sounds (1996). For example, Replace the Letter is an easy-to-implement word game that can be played in individualized sessions, with small groups, or as a whole class.

Replace the Letter Game

1. Present the letters *at* as a word family, showing *at* in a sample word, such as *bat*.

2. Tell students to replace the *b* with an *r*.

3. Ask, "What's the new word?" and allow students to respond. You can choose to have students answer chorally as a class or discuss in small groups or pairs and then share individually. (Answer: *rat*)

Many other appealing activities help young children develop phonemic awareness and phonics skills, such as using children's names to highlight similarities and differences in letters and sounds.

What Do You Notice?

1. Choose pairs of names, such as Joseph and Joanne.

2. Have students notice how they look and sound alike at the beginning.

3. Then, have students notice how they differ in the middle and end.

Another way to teach phonics is for the teacher to explain letters and their sounds when children ask questions about a word. For example, "This word begins with /b/ as in *boy*; this word begins with /g/ as in *girl*, or this word begins with /d/ as in *dinosaur.*"

Sorting activities are excellent for teaching phonemic awareness and phonics skills. Students can play games that require them to sort pictures into categories based on their beginning, middle, or ending sounds, or categorize words with the same rhyme families, vowel generalizations, or other language patterns. This kind of word sorting is an absorbing, purposeful, hands-on activity that requires analytical and critical thinking about language (Strickland 2011).

Teaching Older Students Basic Skills

During the primary grades, most students master phonemic awareness, decoding, and basic word recognition. However, some students are unable to master these basic skills by the end of second grade (Snow, Burns, and Griffin 1998). Students who have difficulty with these foundational skills will likely have difficulty reading and understanding the challenging content-area texts in the intermediate and upper grades. For this reason, teachers are faced with a difficult challenge: How can they provide older students in grades 3–8 or above with effective instruction in word recognition and decoding skills without holding them back from the content that their peers are learning? What should teachers do to help older students read well when standard phonics approaches haven't worked?

To address this issue, I developed a strategy for teaching my own struggling students to decode longer, more challenging multisyllabic words when I was a reading specialist in a New York public school. My approach is called the Syllabication for Decoding Strategy (SDS) (Fink 2006; Fink and Samuels 2008). SDS is a strategy that uses sound, rhythm, and finger or foot movement to help students tap, hear, feel, and write the "beats" in syllables as a way into decoding long words. It's a lively, engaging technique—using rhythm to approach syllabication for the purpose of decoding. Teachers can use SDS for teaching challenging literary, social studies, science, and mathematics vocabulary, thereby promoting literacy learning across content areas. This approach is especially useful for helping older students, English language learners, and students with autism and other learning challenges meet state and national standards in foundational reading and language skills.

SDS is based on the idea that older students can learn to decode longer, multisyllabic words in challenging texts by learning to divide each word at a "sensible syllable break" (Fink 2006; Fink and Samuels 2008). The "sensible syllable break" does not necessarily have to fit with the standard rules of syllabication. Rather, the teacher accepts any break (or syllable division) that helps students divide parts of words into segments in order to pronounce them. Students are guided to divide words into sensible segments or chunks, sound out each chunk, pronounce the word, and indicate how many beats (or syllables) they hear. Then, students learn the meaning of each new word. Figure 2.1 outlines the step-by-step approach of SDS.

The Syllabication for Decoding Strategy is effective not only for English language arts; it can also be used with any content-area words to support learning in science, mathematics, and social studies/history.

Figure 2.1 The Syllabication for Decoding Strategy Protocol

1. As if beating a drum, the teacher taps a desk or table according to the syllables in the teacher's name and in each student's name. Students do the same and guess the number of taps (or syllables) they hear. For example: Ros/a/lie Fink (4); Ma/ry Ken/ne/dy (5); John Smith (2).

2. The teacher selects and writes words on the board or chart paper from students' most challenging reading assignments (e.g., social studies or science). Words should be underlined by the teacher and written in a phrase or sentence in order to place them in a meaningful context.

3. Students attempt syllabication of each word for decoding purposes by drawing a line between letters to show each new beat (or syllable). The syllable divisions do not necessarily have to follow dictionary rules of syllabication. Syllable divisions are accepted as correct for decoding purposes if they help enable students to pronounce the word. For example, if a social studies book includes the word *civilization*, the teacher would accept the following divisions: ci/vi/li/za/tion or civ/i/liz/a/tion or civ/il/iz/a/tion.

4. Students write in parentheses the number of beats or syllables heard in each name or word. For example: ci/vi/li/za/tion (5); A/mer/i/can (4); pho/to/syn/the/sis (5); gene (1); ba/cil/li (3).

5. After pronouncing a word, students guess its meaning from the context or look up the meaning in a dictionary. The teacher explains that SDS is primarily for decoding purposes, and that traditional rules of syllabication have more constraints.

The Syllabication for Decoding Strategy Protocol is useful for lessons on literary terminology and other content-area vocabulary. It's especially helpful for students who struggle with decoding and fluency. Teachers can follow the step-by-step protocol (Figure 2.1) to help students meet goals in decoding and vocabulary knowledge. For students who are uncomfortable tapping loudly, the teacher can suggest that they tap gently under their desks so that nobody can see or hear them.

Teaching Academic Vocabulary

Studies show that students who analyze their own vocabulary knowledge increase their vocabulary repertoire and develop deeper understandings of new word meanings (Mancilla-Martinez and Lesaux 2011). Consequently, teachers are urged to engage students in self-analysis of their own vocabulary knowledge. It's useful for students to rate their own vocabulary knowledge before, during, and after reading. Here are some steps to follow:

Before Reading

1. Choose salient words from the text and present them in the first column of a four-column table (referred to as the *Rate Your Vocabulary Knowledge* activity sheet, Figure 2.2).

2. Have students individually read the words and approximate meanings by writing their guesses in the second column.

3. In pairs, have students group the words in simple categories and make predictions about the text to follow.

During Reading

1. Tell students to find the selected words as they read.

2. Encourage students to take notes while reading and use the notes when they return to their *Rate Your Vocabulary Knowledge* activity sheets at the end of the reading period.

After Reading

1. Direct students to fill out the third column with the correct definition based on the reading.

2. In the fourth column, have students write and reflect on the difference between their first guess and their final answer about the meaning.

Figure 2.2 Rate Your Vocabulary Knowledge

Vocabulary	My Guess	What I Discovered	What I Learned

Five Principles of Good Vocabulary Instruction

We know that students with strong academic vocabularies are likely to succeed in school (Snow 2010). However, according to Harvard Professor Nonie Lesaux (2013), only 10–15 percent of instructional time is spent on teaching vocabulary in most classrooms. Lesaux urges teachers to spend more time on vocabulary instruction and suggests that teachers follow five principles of good vocabulary instruction in order to maximize the benefits of teaching vocabulary.

1. Teach high-utility academic words.

2. Teach depth of word knowledge (not just simple memorization).

3. Provide direct instruction in word-learning strategies.

4. Teach vocabulary that is anchored in text (not in isolation).

5. Provide students with multiple planned activities in which they actively encounter new words.

The teacher can provide regular opportunities for students to play word-recognition and vocabulary games to ensure sufficient word practice and reinforcement. This is fun and it's an effective way for students to meet state and national reading and vocabulary standards and encounter new vocabulary in multiple contexts. Games also provide the multiple exposures that students need in order to master, internalize, and really "own" new words (Hiebert and Kamil 2005; Tamer 2015). Here are three vocabulary and word-recognition games.

Grab the Word

1. To begin the game, the teacher selects appropriate vocabulary words, writes them on index cards, and displays them on the board.

2. A selected student locates the card containing a word that is read aloud by either the teacher or a student leader.

3. The student then tells the number of syllables or beats in the word and gives a correct definition of the word. Then the student creates a sentence using the word orally.

4. The next student takes a turn and the steps repeat with a new word from the board. This game can also be played in small groups with several sets of cards, one set per group.

Music Makers

1. The teacher provides groups of students (4–6 in a group) with a set of vocabulary words related to a lesson or unit they've been studying.

2. The students make up a song or rap that uses the words in context. They must use the language accurately as they create their lyrics.

3. Students practice reading/chanting their raps rhythmically in unison; then each group performs for the whole class.

Chart and Match

1. The teacher displays the vocabulary words on the board or document camera.

2. The students create a three-column grid with the following headings: Word; Illustration or Example; and Definition or Description. The students write the vocabulary words down the left side of the grid, one word per row.

3. The students then draw pictures or examples in the center column to illustrate the vocabulary words.

4. In the final column, the teacher and students engage in a discussion to create definitions for all of the words. This should not be a dictionary definition; rather, it should be one that everyone agrees upon and creates together. Students then record the definitions on their grids.

5. After reviewing their finished grids, students cut apart the squares.

6. Students then walk around the room with their pieces and trade cards with others around the room to end up with a mixture of cards from different classmates.

7. Students finally recreate their charts using their new pieces.

Pre-Teaching New Vocabulary

Researchers have found that when students are pre-taught new word meanings *before* they read a text, they understand and remember new vocabulary better and improve their comprehension and recall of challenging content concepts (Mancilla-Martinez and Lesaux 2011; Snow 2010). Therefore, it's a good idea to pre-teach new vocabulary before reading. Pre-teaching vocabulary techniques work well for teaching a whole class, a small group, or individual students. Here are steps to take with primary grade students:

1. Pre-select one new vocabulary word each day from a narrative or informational text to teach meaning from context.

2. Before reading the text aloud, introduce the text and read aloud the entire sentence with the new vocabulary word. Tell the class which new vocabulary word has been selected.

3. Say, "While I read you the story (or informational book), listen carefully and try to guess the meaning of _____ as it is used in this story."

4. Explain that the words and sentences near the new vocabulary word usually give clues or hints about the word's meaning.

5. While reading the text aloud, stop at the new word.

6. In pairs, have students guess and discuss the likely meaning of the new word based on the surrounding words and sentences.

7. Have students share their guesses. (Alternately, this can be done as a whole class or in a small group.)

8. Ask students what they think the new word means and have them share the specific clues they used from the text to make their guesses.

9. Confirm the correct word meaning. (If students guess incorrectly, say, "That was a good/smart guess, but in this case the word means _____.")

In addition to pre-teaching vocabulary to young children, it's equally important to pre-teach new vocabulary to older students, especially since academic vocabulary has been shown to contribute vitally to their ultimate success (Snow 2010). Some ways to implement this approach for older students in grades 3 and above, are outlined here:

1. Select 5–10 new vocabulary words that students will need to know in order to understand the new text.

2. Present the new vocabulary words in phrases or sentences taken directly from the text, or create your own sentences that use the new vocabulary words in a way relevant to your students.

3. Underline the new vocabulary word(s) in each sentence or phrase, simultaneously pointing to and reading the sentence aloud to the class.

4. Teach students that the way a word is used in a sentence is called its context.

5. Instruct students to find and underline clues to each word's meaning in the context, or surrounding words and ideas.

6. Invite students to guess the meaning of each new word based on its context, pointing out that contextual guessing is a less time-consuming way to expand vocabulary than looking up words in a dictionary. Explain that contextual guessing should be used in addition to a dictionary.

7. Have students explain their guesses about each new word's meaning and the clues that led to their guesses. Together, discuss the meanings of the words as they are used in the sentences. Accept any synonyms or short definitions that fit with the meanings in order to encourage contextual guessing. If a student guesses a word meaning incorrectly, say, "Good guess, but the word _____ actually means _____." This encourages student effort and active participation, but clarifies the correct meaning, both for the student and for the rest of the class.

In addition to encouraging students to make guesses about possible word meanings based on the context, it helps to familiarize them with the unique language and style of dictionary definitions. One way to do this is by playing The Dictionary Game. This is a hilarious, engaging activity appropriate for students in grades 4 and above; it familiarizes them with new word meanings and the distinctive language unique to dictionaries (called "dictionaryese"). This game can be played by small groups of 3–8 players or by the whole class. Here are instructions for playing The Dictionary Game:

The Dictionary Game

1. Index cards are distributed to each player. A student is selected to be the word chooser, after ample modeling by the teacher.

2. The word chooser looks up a word in a dictionary and copies the word and its exact meaning(s). After a word has been chosen, the word is read aloud with its definition hidden.

3. Each student then writes a made-up definition of the word, attempting to write in "dictionaryese"—the distinctive linguistic style of dictionary definitions, including part of speech, derivation, and etymology (history of the word).

4. After each player has created a written definition, the chooser collects all of the index cards with the made-up definitions.

5. The chooser then reads each definition aloud one-by-one, including the actual dictionary definition, without indicating which one is correct. As the definitions are read aloud, the other players raise their hands when they think they hear the real definition. The teacher keeps track of the number of players who raise their hands for each definition.

6. The chooser then reads the real definition of the word aloud so that everyone learns the real meaning of the new word.

7. The person who wrote the most convincing (yet false) definition that attracted the most raised hands is the winner.

Teaching Close Reading of Complex Texts

State and national standards emphasize close reading of complex, challenging texts. According to Timothy Shanahan (2012), the teacher's role in close reading is mainly that of facilitator or "Guide in Chief." Students are expected to grapple with the text and figure it out in multiple ways: independently, with teacher guidance, and with peers. Interactive aspects of close reading discussions can be intellectually stimulating and promote deep understanding.

Stephanie Harvey's interpretation of close reading focuses on the teacher's role in choosing noteworthy, important books that delve into complex, multifaceted issues that really matter in today's world (Harvey 2015). Harvey urges teachers to focus on big ideas that really matter and choose texts for their importance in real life—including texts that address difficult subjects (e.g., bullying or racism). To maximize the benefits of close reading, teachers need to choose challenging, high-interest texts with literary merit that capture the attention of most students—male and female, affluent and disadvantaged, English language learners, gifted students, typically developing learners, and students with learning disabilities. Close reading usually involves multiple readings of the same text accompanied by lots of discussion.

In addition to focusing on close reading, recent research emphasizes the importance of providing students with frequent experiences reading informational texts, beginning in PreK and kindergarten and continuing throughout the grades (Duke and Pearson 2002; Duke et al. 2011; Duke 2013). This is because frequent early experiences with informational texts enhance a student's chances of academic success later on in life (Duke 2013; Duke et. al. 2011). Consequently, it's never too early to use informational texts.

Bullies Are a Pain in the Brain by Trevor Romain (1997) is an outstanding choice for a close reading. It treats bullying in a way that students of all backgrounds can relate to easily, regardless of whether they see themselves as bullies, victims, bystanders, or upstanders. It has humorous illustrations and lots of useful information, including role-plays and five myths about bullies. This story is a read-aloud for young students, but by third grade, most can read the book independently or in pairs with a reading buddy.

A Process for Close Reading

In a close reading, teachers select a text and read it aloud or have students read it independently or in pairs, depending on the students' instructional needs. Then, students can engage in multiple readings. Here are suggestions for guiding students' first reading, second reading, and third reading of a text, as well as sample questions to use with each reading. Some questions are text dependent, while others are more open-ended.

First Reading

A key feature of the first close reading is that students initially read the text independently before discussing it. The first reading focuses primarily on comprehending the text at a basic level with questions such as:

- What are the conflicts and how are the conflicts resolved? How do you know?

- What are two things that you learned on page _____? How do you feel about what you learned?

Second Reading

In the second reading students explore how the text worked and the techniques the author used. Students should be encouraged to explore deeper-level questions and support their responses with evidence from the text. In some cases, it may be appropriate for students to reread only selected salient passages of the text. Some possible questions to ask are:

- How did the author organize this text?

- What literary devices did the author use and how effective were they?

- What was the quality of the evidence in this book?

- What does the word _____ mean as it is used on page _____ ? Why do you think the author used the word here in this way?

- What is the meaning of the term _____ according to the author? Is the term _____ used consistently in the same way throughout the book, or does its meaning change?

- What do you think the author means on page _____ when he/she writes _____ ? How do you know?

- What was the most important thing you learned from reading this book? Why is it important to you?

- How have your feelings and thoughts about _____ changed?

- What were the characters like?

- What kinds of relationships were evident among the characters?

- Did the characters develop and change? If so, how did they change? How do you know? What evidence in the text suggests this?

- Did any of the characters remain static? If so, how do you know? What evidence in the text suggests this?

- What examples and explanations does the author include in this book? How effective do you think the examples and explanations are? Why?

Third Reading

The third reading provides an opportunity to explore major themes and deeper meanings of the text. The following questions can help navigate meaningful discussions characteristic of a third reading.

- What is the overarching meaning of this book? For example, what is the theme and what are some of the main ideas?

- What is the author's point of view? Does the author's point of view differ from the point of view of the narrator? If so, how does it differ? How do you know? What evidence suggests this difference?

- In what ways does the book relate to you?

- How does this book/text relate to other short stories or books you've read or movies you've seen?

- How would you evaluate _____ aesthetically? What elements of beauty does the book contain?

- Would you recommend this book to a friend or relative? Why?

As a follow-up activity, young students can role-play based on a compelling vignette or turning point in the book. Older students can work collaboratively in small groups, writing a Reader's Theater script and performing it for the rest of the class. (See Reader's Theater Protocol in Chapter 3 for step-by-step instructions.)

Using Rhythm Walks/Dances for Repeated Reading

Rhythm Walks/Dances are exciting, highly motivating activities that use walking, dancing, and body movement to support fluency development, an important foundational reading skill. They provide opportunities for intensive instruction in repeated reading, a method found to be key to fluency success for all types of students (Fink and Samuels 2008; Samuels 2006). As students repeat the Rhythm Walk or Dance, they increasingly use gesture, intonation, and expression to convey meaning. The result is an elaborate line dance that motivates students to read and simultaneously builds fluency and joyful reading.

Pairing skilled readers with less skilled readers who walk, sway, and read in unison is an excellent way to use Rhythm Walks/ Dances to support English language learners and students with learning disabilities (Chard, Vaughn, and Tyler 2002). Figure 2.3 shows steps for conducting a Rhythm Walk/Dance. Before beginning this activity, the teacher can model the process for students. Rhythm Walks/Dances can be used for a whole class, small groups, or partners, who sway together rhythmically.

Figure 2.3 Steps for Conducting a Rhythm Walk/Dance

1. Have the class choose a short poem, story, or informational text.

2. Analyze the text; decide where there are natural breaks of phrases or sentences through punctuation, line breaks, or context clues.

3. Write each "chunk" of text on a large rectangular cardboard strip, writing in large letters (about an inch and a half high).

4. Place strips in order—either in a curved or straight pathway on the floor. Each strip should be a distance of one child-size step away from the next strip.

5. Have students line up in single file.

6. The first student reads the first strip aloud, then steps to the next strip of text, reads this aloud, and so on until completing the passage. To add movement, have students sway from side to side, bending slightly at the waist as they walk. This creates an undulating line dance in swaying motion.

7. Each student begins when the student in front has completed the first three strips.

8. When students reach the end of the Rhythm Walk, they line up at the beginning and begin the process again (3–10 times).

9. To facilitate comprehension, the teacher can conclude the lesson with response journal writing and discussion questions.

(Adapted from Peebles 2007)

Teaching Critical Literacy

Critical literacy is a guided approach to reading and writing that cultivates deep understanding of complex texts. Students analyze their assumptions about the world by questioning the author's and their own assumptions about gender, race, religion, nationality, ethnicity, and socioeconomic class. With critical literacy, students gain insights into the complexities and nuances of social relationships, insights that help them forge their own evolving identities (Bean 2009). Critical literacy strategies are based on highly motivating, interesting discussion question protocols that are open-ended and easily modified to meet the developmental needs of students at different grade levels. These types of questions help facilitate engaging discussions that lead to rich writing experiences and meet current literacy goals in speaking, listening, reading, and writing. Here are some examples (Adapted from Harper and Bean 2003):

Fairy Tales (Grades K–2)

- What do you think is meant by, "They lived happily ever after?" Do you like this type of ending? Why?

- What do you think the main characters' lives were like later? Do you think they were happy? Why?

- What do you think the boy's life was like? What do you think the girl's life was like? Why?

- How fulfilling or happy were their lives? Why?

- How might the story have differed if the villain were the winner instead?

Fairy Tales (Grades K–2) *(cont.)*

- Did you like the book's ending? Why? How would you change the ending if you were the author? Why would you change it in this way?

- Did any of your ideas change after reading this book? How? Did they change as a result of reading and/or as a result of listening to your classmates' interpretations and opinions? Explain.

Novels (Grades 3 and Above)

- What character do you like most? Why?

- How is this character like you? In what ways are his or her experiences similar to yours? Give examples. How do they differ from your experiences? Explain.

- What is the main character's role in the plot of this story? Explain.

- Which characters have the most power? Which characters have the least power? How do you know?

- Which characters are unseen or have no voice? Why?

- What view(s) of the world do we see through the narrator? Do you agree with this view? Why?

- How do characters in this book compare to other characters you have read about, seen, or heard in books, magazines, video games, websites, TV, music, movies, conversations, or advertisements?

Novels (Grades 3 and Above) *(cont.)*

- What did you learn from reading this book? What else would you like to learn about this topic?

- Did you like the book's ending? Why? How would you change the ending if you were the author? Why would you change it in this way? How could your plot change or alter the author's message?

- What, if anything, annoys or angers you about this book? Why? How would you change this aspect of the story?

- How do you think your parents, relatives, or members of your church, synagogue, or mosque would feel about this book?

- Why do you think the author wrote this book? What was the author's purpose? Did he or she succeed? How?

- What is the theme of the book?

In addition to using teacher-devised discussion questions, students can create their own critical literacy questions individually or by working in pairs, small groups, or as a whole class. Devising their own critical literacy questions helps students analyze complex texts and become more engaged and excited about reading, thinking, and writing (Harper and Bean 2003). Critical literacy can also be cultivated through writing activities. Teachers can give students choices to select a writing activity based on their own personal interests. For example, teachers can encourage students to give voice to a minor character who was silent in the original text and ask them to retell, rewrite, or dramatize the events or outcome of a story through the eyes of the minor character. Here are some ideas:

Grades K-2

Ask students to read *The Three Little Pigs* and then write about what the mother of the three little pigs thinks about her sons' encounters with the world.

Grades 3-5

Have students rewrite parts of *Sarah, Plain and Tall* by Patricia MacLachlan to show what Papa thought about Sarah and her suitability for the family.

Students can also put themselves in the role of a major character and imagine and discuss how they would feel if they were that character.

Secondary

Have students imagine themselves as Farah in *The Story of My Life: An Afghan Girl on the Other Side of the Sky* by Farah Ahmedi. Students can describe Farah's situation at key points and places in the story—in Afghanistan, in Germany, and finally in the United States. Have students discuss how they would feel as Farah in different countries. What challenges does Farah face at each point and how does she negotiate each challenge? How might you have reacted differently if you were Farah? Explain.

(Adapted from Prosenjak 1999)

Teaching Language Arts through Rhythm

Teaching with Rap

Rap is an exciting medium for immersing students in reading and writing. Teachers can encourage students to compose raps of their own, as well as other forms of poetry on topics of personal interest. Creating their own raps helps students develop the ability to use intricate language, multiple word meanings, enticing rhythms, and interesting sounds to express meaning. Rap is a wonderful tool for teaching literature, especially when students create their own original lyrics. Not only is rap fun, but it also provides students with an opportunity to reflect, review, and write about what they learn from reading complex texts.

For example, use texts that provide opportunities for reflection, review, writing, and performing. After students read a selected text, the teacher can guide them to consolidate and review what they learned from the text by following The Rap Protocol found in Chapter 1. The step-by-step guidelines in this protocol are easy to follow and will help students write their own raps about books they read. Creating original raps is engaging and effective for deep reflection, review, and writing about literature. In addition to writing their own raps and poems, students can read and recite raps written by others, such as other classmates or their own teachers.

What Girls Learn by Karin Cook (1997) is a terrific fast-paced novel that is excellent for enrichment and review with student-created raps. This coming of age novel, suitable for middle school and high school students, is about two sisters, ages 11 and 12. It deals with several universal themes, including sibling rivalry, acceptance of a stepfather, illness, and loss. The following are student-created raps about the novel. In addition to composing their raps in small-group activity sessions, students performed them in their English classes. Creating their own raps helped these students synthesize and review a complex text, and deepen their understanding of its multiple meanings. The students enjoyed these experiences immensely, making English class interesting, educational, and fun.

Sibling Rivalry

by Molly Wyman and Michelle Goldberg

We fight about clothes
'Cause you steal my sweaters,
And sometimes we argue
But it's all for the better.

We look out for each other
From dating to looks,
And when you need help
I crack open the books.

Our fights don't last long
Even though they're intense,
We can't stay mad for long
'Cause our love is immense!

Euphemisms, Dark Secrets, White Lies Too

by Todd Neill

In school one day Tilden gets an invitation
To see a movie about menstruation.
She hides the invite 'til the right time to tell
'Cause right about now, Mama isn't doing well.

Her doctor's appointment isn't routine,
She'll be in the hospital a week, it seems.
They learn that Mama has a lump in her breast,
It could be cancer; they'll find out from the test.

Tilden and her sister and Nick are on edge,
They go to visit Mama and stand near her bed.
Tilden gets mad and feels really, really sick
When she learns that Mama told her secret just to Nick.

Euphemisms, dark secrets, white lies too,
They make you feel betrayed and out of the loop.
Euphemisms, omissions, white lies too,
Do they ever really help, or just hurt you?

Writing and performing their own raps helped the students who read *What Girls Learn* engage in a close reading of this challenging novel. It enabled them to examine its complex themes thoughtfully and critically. The process of composing their raps helped them reflect, analyze, and discuss literary elements and ethical dilemmas, deepen their understanding of the book as a whole, and review the themes and meanings embedded in this complex text. Finally, reviewing, writing, and performing the raps for their peers helped the students prepare for a test on the novel. This book deals with several challenging issues in the lives of the novel's two teenage sisters—menstruation, puberty, and sexuality; their complex sisterly relationship; their relationships with their mother and stepfather; their single mother's marriage; their mother's diagnosis of breast cancer; and the untimely death of their young mother. Students learned a lot and enjoyed reading this fast-paced, realistic novel. They learned to analyze and appreciate the author's adept ability to build plot suspense, develop realistic characters, portray dynamic relationships, and pursue important universal themes.

Poetry

Another literary genre that provides rich opportunities for learning in language arts is poetry. An interesting way to help students understand poetry and integrate it into their own lives is to have them choose a poem that they like, then write a poem of their own based on the style and structure of the poem they selected. The style and structure remain the same, but the subject matter is the student's own. This is an excellent way for students to express their own ideas and feelings through creative poems of their own making. They not only develop knowledge of poetic forms but also genuine pride in their own literary creations. The following are original poems by first grader Maya Feldman and third graders Ben Feldman and Alisa Feldman. They were inspired by the poetry of Robert Louis Stevenson and other poets.

I Am the Moon

by Ben Feldman

I am the Moon
A shiny laffy taffy
Singing with the stars
Twinkling like sour patches.

White Is

by Ben Feldman

White is my sister's
Toast across the room.
White is as sweet as buttery
Mint ready for me.
White is a tasty cream puff
Waiting on a plate.
White is a glow from the clouds.
White is a dog
Waiting for someone to buy him.

Mountain Climbing

by Ben Feldman

When you climb a mountain, you might see a lot of
amazing things
The sun cooks up the top of the mountain.
It creates gray, dark orange strips and covers the
mountain
Like a blanket. I see a tall peak as pointy as a thumb-
tack.
The blue sky is dripping through the mountains. Its
aquamarine color shines out at me.
I can taste the fresh air at the top of the mountain. I
hear gray and orange rough rocks
Crumbling beneath my feet. Smooth bumps at
The bottom of the mountain
Feel like gumdrops.
Sand whooshes in my ear.

Ice Skating

by Maya Feldman

Good one-foot spirals are
Fun to do.
The ice is very slippery,
Noisy and scratchy.
Perfect edges you have to
Learn.
Ice-skating is wonderful!

Who Is Alisa?

by Alisa Feldman

Lively, athletic, amazing,
Wishes to be in the circus
When she grows up.

Dreams of having a pet
Elephant named George.

Wants to be the best soccer
Player in the world.

Wonders why she must
Go to school.

Students can learn from basing their own original poems on famous models. This was the case with "Imprisoned Boy" by seventh grader Ben Feldman. Ben composed his original poem based on "Caged Bird" by Nobel laureate Maya Angelou. Ben's English teacher instructed the class to write an original poem on a topic of interest, using the format and structure of Maya Angelou's poem. After completing "Imprisoned Boy," Ben was so proud of his accomplishment that he wrote, "P.S. I made it on my own!"

Imprisoned Boy

by Ben Feldman

The carefree boy
Runs through the forest,
The scent of pine
All around,
Eating candy,
Pound after pound.

But a boy who
Walks in his cell
Can almost smell
The scent of freedom.

His hands are cuffed
And his every move
Is being watched,
So he cries for his family,
Cries for his family.

The imprisoned boy cries,
Scared of his narrow path,
For the things he needs to have.
He cries so long
That the guards come along
And deprive him of his pride.

The carefree boy horses around
And wanders through the forest,
Finds a dollar bill,
Lying on the hill,
And then he pays
For a horseback ride.

But the imprisoned boy
Stands on the brink of despair
So sad he can barely breathe the air
His hands are cuffed
And his every move is being watched
So he cries for his family,
Cries for his family.

The imprisoned boy cries,
Scared of his narrow path,
For the things he needs to have.
He cries so long
That the guards come along
And deprive him of his pride.
They deprive him of his pride.

   Another way to engage students in writing poetry is to have
them write poems based on diaries and other primary sources.
This kind of poetry writing is both interesting and challenging.
It enhances students' understanding of complex texts, provides

authentic experiences using primary sources, and promotes the development of sophisticated writing skills from various perspectives. Sharing their work with a partner, small group, whole class, or a broader audience, such as the whole school or family members, provides even deeper engagement and motivation for writing.

Students' personal journals are an exciting way to engage them in writing poetry. After writing a prose entry on a topic of interest (such as an interesting weekend adventure, an experience with a friend or relative, or a favorite hobby), students can create an original poem based on their entries. The teacher guides students by offering choices about the type of poem and provides examples of different types of poems, including couplets, diamante, cinquain, and Haiku.

Two poetry resources with lots of examples for teachers and students are:

- *A Child's Anthology of Poetry* edited by Elizabeth Hauge Sword
- *Talking to the Sun: An Illustrated Anthology of Poems for Young People* edited by Kenneth Koch and Kate Farrell

Celebrating Poetry with Festivals

Poetry festivals—and celebrations for other genres, too—are great ways for students to share favorite texts and original writing. Festivals can use two formats. In the first format, students "perform" by reciting favorite poems by famous poets. This can be enhanced with personally selected toys, gestures, songs, dances, videos, and props. In the second format, students perform self-written poems on topics of personal interest. Each reading is followed by a share session with the author, which includes immediate feedback from classmates and members of the audience. In addition to performing, students can also display their poems or other written work on bulletin boards or on school websites.

I observed a poetry festival in Evie Weinstein-Parks' fourth-grade class. The students wrote and recited original poems about a range of topics, including riding a two-wheeler for the first time, emulating a baseball star at bat, frolicking with a pet in the grass, feeling ambivalent about a brother or sister, and feeling sad about a grandparent's death.

During their poetry performances, the students' enthusiasm was contagious, and each family's delight in their child's accomplishment was palpable. Ms. Weinstein-Parks' students were fully engaged in all aspects of the festival—reading, writing, performing, and discussing their work with the audience. This capstone event helped Ms. Weinstein-Parks' students meet literacy goals in reading, writing, speaking, and listening as they celebrated their literary accomplishments.

Using Reader's Theater

Reader's Theater provides a highly motivating, creative literacy experience for students while meeting state and national standards in reading, writing, and oral presentation skills. This creative approach is great for developing several key literacy skills simultaneously: fluency, comprehension, writing, speaking, and listening (Fredericks 2011). A Reader's Theater approach emphasizes vivid oral reading and accurate interpretation of lines. Students do not memorize scripts; instead, they read aloud and concentrate on voice interpretation, characterization, and reading fluency. Reader's Theater provides practice in oral reading and communication of meaning through voice intonation, expression, cadence, and speed. Students perform with the script in hand, while the audience (comprised of fellow class members) listens, provides feedback, and sometimes improvises endings.

By engaging students in short, dramatic scenes from great literary works, Reader's Theater can inspire students to read an entire literary work afterwards (Fredericks 2011). This lively, creative approach is appropriate for students of all ages, levels, and interests. It can be especially beneficial for struggling readers and English language learners because it sets a purpose for repeated reading—performance. When students practice reading the text over and over again in preparation for the performance, it supports their fluency, prosody, overall language development, and confidence as readers. For English language learners, it can also be an opportunity to enhance identity development and cultural pride when the topics chosen support their heritage. This can contribute to their overall academic success (Fink 2006). For example, Reader's Theater enactments can be turned into multicultural literacy experiences by using scripts based on folk tales from across the globe.

An outstanding Reader's Theater website is Aaron Shepard's Reader's Theater Page at www.aaronshep.com/rt/.

Creating Reader's Theater Scripts

In addition to using commercial Reader's Theater scripts, teachers can guide students to write and perform their own scripts. This can be done in small groups of about 3–6 students. Here are steps for guiding students to write their own Reader's Theater scripts.

Figure 2.4 Reader's Theater Protocol

1. After the teacher divides the class into small groups of 3–6 students, each group chooses a favorite fairy tale, narrative, or informational text.

2. Each group selects a favorite portion, or vignette, from the text and chooses one person to be the scribe.

3. Each group decides to do one of the following:
   - Rewrite a favorite portion as a dramatic script with dialogue and action.
   - Rewrite a dramatic script with a different ending from the story's actual ending.

4. The group creates a script that includes a part for a narrator and each group member. The script includes dialogue, gestures, and action. Sound effects may also be included.

5. A person chosen as the scribe writes what the whole group decides on and makes copies as needed.

6. After the group finishes writing, they practice reading the script aloud. The teacher encourages students to "ham it up" and be dramatic by using expressive intonation, body language, gesture, and movement or dance to help convey meaning. Note: Scarves can be used to encourage body motion and to indicate costumes, props, and scenery.

7. After practicing the script aloud a few times, each group performs its creative Reader's Theater script for an audience (the rest of the class, another peer-level class, a younger class, a school assembly, or a parent group).

Reader's Theater Resources

Grades K–2

How and Why Stories for Reader's Theatre by Judy Wolfman

Take a Quick Bow: 26 Short Plays for Classroom Fun by Pamela Marx

The Lost Cat: and Other Primary Plays for Oral Reading by Ann R. Talbot

Grades 3–4

Just Deal with It! Funny Reader's Theater for Life's Not-So-Funny Moments by Diana R. Jenkins

Reader's Theater for Building Fluency: Strategies and Scripts for Making the Most of this Highly Effective, Motivating, and Research-Based Approach to Oral Reading by Jo Worthy

Reader's Theater for Children: Scripts and Script Development by Mildred Knight Laughlin and Kathy Howard Latrobe

Silly Salamanders and Other Slightly Stupid Stuff for Reader's Theatre by Anthony D. Fredericks

Social Studies Reader's Theatre for Children: Scripts and Script Development by Mildred Knight Laughlin, Peggy Tubbs Black, and Margery Kirby Loberg

Grades 5–8

Live on Stage: Teacher Resource Book, Performing Arts for Middle School by Carla Blank and Jody Roberts

Reader's Theater for Young Adults: Script and Script Development by Mildred Knight Laughlin and Kathy Howard Latrobe

Shattering the Myth: Plays by Hispanic Women by Cherrie Moraga, Migdalia Cruz, Caridad Svich, Josephia Lopez, Edit Villareal, Diana Saenz, Linda Feyder, and Denise Chavez

Using Visual Art

Art provides an intriguing springboard for teaching many English language arts skills: observation, listening, speaking, and writing. For example, to prepare for a descriptive expository writing activity using visual art, the teacher can bring in paintings, prints, and picture postcards to display. To begin the art writing activity, tell students to observe the items carefully, noticing as many details as possible. Then, have students describe each work of art by writing as many rich, descriptive details as possible based on what they see. The attention to detail in this approach strengthens students' writing ability while emphasizing the skills of observing and articulating details. The teacher can easily transform this activity into an art writing guessing game as well.

The Art Writing Guessing Game (Grades 3 and Above)

1. The teacher collects various art prints, one per student. (Note: If locating art prints is difficult or expensive, picture postcards are equally effective.)

2. The teacher displays the artwork in a visible spot in the room, and each student selects one print and takes it to his or her seat.

3. The teacher tells students that in order to play this art writing game, they need to look carefully at their prints and notice as many details as possible about the colors, shapes, designs, light, topics, painting styles, or techniques. (Note: The teacher explains that students do not need to be "good artists" or know a lot about painting; they simply need to write a detailed description of what they see in the picture.)

4. Students write as quickly as possible and include all the details they notice.

5. When students have finished writing, they place their sheets of paper upside down in a pile on a desk in the center of the room. The teacher mixes up the sheets and each student then selects a sheet with a description on it.

6. Each student takes a turn reading one description aloud to the class or small group. The other students listen to the reader and, as soon as they think they can locate the picture being described, they raise their hands and point to the painting.

7. The first student to locate a painting correctly gets to keep that painting until the end of the game. The winner is the student who correctly identifies the most paintings.

The Portfolio Edition of *The Mysteries of Harris Burdick* by Chris Van Allsburg contains large black and white prints that portray a variety of subjects and settings. It's a useful tool to engage students in The Art Writing Guessing Game.

The Art Writing Guessing Game can easily be modified for students in grades K–2 as an exciting speaking and listening activity. Here is a K–2 adaptation:

The Art Writing Guessing Game (Grades K–2)

1. The teacher collects various art prints, one per student. (Note: If locating art prints is difficult or expensive, picture postcards are equally effective.)

2. The teacher displays the artwork in a visible spot in the room, and each student selects one print and takes it to his or her seat.

3. Students look at their artwork carefully and observe and think about the details of what they see.

4. Students return their art print for display by leaning it upright on the chalkboard or whiteboard ledge. They orally describe the details of their artwork aloud to the class.

5. When the students listening to the description think they know which picture is being described, they raise their hands and point to the artwork being described when called on by the teacher.

6. The first student to locate a painting correctly gets to keep that painting until the end of the game. The winner is the student who correctly identifies the most paintings.

This activity helps hone young students' observation, speaking, and listening skills—important goals of the new state and national standards.

Using Writing Conferences

Students benefit enormously from active participation in peer writing conferences after they write expository essays, narrative stories, raps, poems, or any other genre. Writing conferences can be held in short, 15-minute share sessions (Graves 1994). During peer sharing sessions, guide students to do the following:

- read their written work aloud

- listen carefully to one another reading

- give and receive constructive feedback, which is useful for revising and editing

Teaching with this interactive writing process approach involves lots of peer sharing and feedback. It helps students develop skills and confidence as writers and is appropriate across ages and grade levels. Students find this writing process approach extremely helpful and remark on its continuing usefulness to them as writers. This is an excellent way for teachers to help students meet listening, speaking, and writing goals of the Common Core and other state and national standards. Figure 2.5 shows a useful protocol for all types of writing. The protocol emphasizes the use of sharing and constructive feedback.

Figure 2.5 Writing Share Session Protocol

1. **Listen:** The writer reads his or her poem, rap, or essay aloud while others listen.

2. **Remember:** The listener tells the writer everything that he or she remembers from listening or retells the part of the poem (or other genre) that he or she likes best and explains why.

3. **Remind:** The listener tells the writer that this piece of writing reminds the listener of another story or another poem. This encourages students to make text-to-text connections, enhancing comprehension.

4. **Stand Out**: The listener tells the writer what was most striking about the piece. For example, "What stood out for me was...." A student may comment on a vignette, a theme, or a vivid word and its part of speech or meaning.

5. **Question:** The listener asks the writer a specific question for clarification. This questioning helps the writer pinpoint what is unclear and needs revision.

(Adapted from Graves 1994)

The Research, Decide, Teach Approach

Writing conferences are extremely effective for providing individualized writing guidance and specific feedback. A recent addition to the traditional conference format is an effective strategy called the Research, Decide, Teach Approach. This strategy results in more focused, productive conferences. The key here is for the teacher to informally assess what the student needs to learn and then teach that one skill during the conference. The following shows how to implement each step in this writing conference strategy, adapted by Holly and Mary McMackin (2013) from the more traditional conference approach. (Note: While the teacher conducts individual writing conferences, the other students work quietly on their own writing projects.)

1. **Research:** The teacher uses information from records and previous interactions with the student and carefully observes the student's reading and writing behavior. Then the teacher records the student's specific reading and writing strengths and challenges.

2. **Decide:** The teacher decides on one specific aspect of writing that needs improvement and selects this aspect as the focus of the conference.

3. **Teach.** The teacher gives explicit instruction, models, and teaches the skill that is the focus of instruction in this conference session.

Conclusion

Teachers can promote successful reading and writing for all types of students through rigorous, focused, coherent literacy instruction that is both challenging and exciting. By integrating rap, poetry, drama, visual art, and creative movement with a variety of English language arts activities, teachers add a novel dimension that reinforces and enriches traditional approaches. Innovative use of the arts and multisensory, hands-on activities inspire excitement and fascination about English language arts, enabling students to master key skills in reading and writing. By infusing language arts lessons with captivating activities, enticing materials, and effective strategies, teachers can inspire students of all backgrounds and abilities and promote success for all.

Reflect and Discuss

1. What excites you most from this chapter? Why?

2. What strategy or activity do you plan to implement in an upcoming lesson? What do you need to do to prepare for this?

3. Think about the strategy or activity that you selected in the previous question. What potential challenges do you anticipate? How could these be addressed?

4. How could the activities and materials shared in this chapter help your students develop their literacy skills while simultaneously meeting state and national literacy goals?

Chapter 3

Reading, Writing, and Rhythm in Science

Questions to Activate Thinking

1. What aspects of teaching science are most interesting and rewarding for you?

2. What are the biggest challenges you face today in teaching science?

3. What role does content-area literacy play in your current science instruction?

4. How do you address the learning of new science vocabulary with students?

Meeting Next Generation Science and Literacy Standards

Next Generation Science Standards (NGSS Lead States 2013) emphasize scientific observation, speaking, listening, and reading (National Research Council 2012). In addition, the new science standards extend the breadth and depth of science writing experiences, hands-on activities, and experimentation. Taken together, these changes in science teaching are exciting, yet they present significant new challenges. How can teachers tackle the new challenges and promote scientific literacy and enthusiasm for science?

This chapter addresses this question through highly engaging science activities, strategies, and materials that aim to motivate, inspire, and instruct students in scientific literacy. The purpose of this chapter is to get students excited and enthusiastic about learning science as they develop increasingly sophisticated science vocabulary, knowledge, and skills.

Teaching Scientific Literacy through Reading

One extremely effective way to promote scientific literacy is to include reading as a regular component of science lessons. This is easily accomplished by following a systematic sequence for teaching with science texts that includes overviewing and previewing the text prior to reading. Overviews and previews have been shown to be effective for increasing students' understanding and memory of all kinds of informational texts, including science texts (Duke 2013; Duke and Pearson 2002; Pauk and Owens 2011).

To conduct systematic overviews and previews, the teacher begins by guiding students to survey the text *prior to reading it*. Next, the teacher guides students to create their own questions based on the title, pictures, and boldfaced headings. In addition, the teacher also presents new science vocabulary in context before students read the text.

Here are seven steps for presenting a new science text. These steps can be used for most science texts, regardless of the topic. They are a good way to promote students' literacy development and meet state and national standards for increasing skills in vocabulary knowledge, reading, writing, speaking, and listening. The seven steps include activities before, during, and after reading.

Before Reading

1. The teacher directs students to survey the title, pictures, and bold headings of the text/chapter.

2. Younger students ask questions orally about the title, each picture, and each bold heading. Older students write down their questions.

3. The teacher pre-teaches science vocabulary in meaningful phrases or sentences taken from the chapter.

4. The teacher creates a clear purpose for reading the text and states it explicitly. For example, "Read to find out how scientists created a vaccine to prevent polio," or "Read to find out why Pluto is no longer considered a planet."

During Reading

5. Students and/or the teacher ask three different types of comprehension questions—factual, inferential, and critical thinking/open-ended questions.

After Reading

6. The teacher provides regular opportunities for students to discuss their responses to questions and their reactions to the text. For example, after reading a new chapter, students use Turn and Talk activities with partners or small groups.

7. The teacher and/or students create engaging, enriching, hands-on activities that involve a wide variety of experiences for each science lesson, such as writing, acting, singing, moving, drawing, painting, sculpting, and designing and conducting experiments.

In addition to using science texts throughout the course of lessons or units, it's important to encourage students to read science texts outside of structured instruction. A great way to facilitate students' reading about their science interests is to create a science library in every classroom. Science libraries enable students to read complex science texts, including "stretch" texts in a high-grade level band with appropriate scaffolding.

Stretch texts are complex texts of interest to students. They are both engaging and challenging. The teacher's role is to help individual students select appropriate stretch texts, which may be above the student's instructional reading level yet are of interest to the student. With teacher scaffolding, the student can comprehend the stretch text and increase his or her overall reading ability. (Note: Kindergarten and first grade teachers can read informational science texts aloud to the class, while older students can read these texts independently. High-quality science trade books for students on a variety of topics are presented in Appendix C.)

Two professional resources that delve deeply into stretch texts are:

- *Teaching Students to Closely Read Texts: How and When?* by Diane Lapp
- "What's Complex in Text Complexity?" by Elfrieda Hiebert

Setting Explicit Purposes for Reading Science

Effective science lessons are purpose-driven and revolve around learning specific science concepts. When teachers set explicit purposes for reading a new science text, it helps students to do the following:

- focus their attention
- get actively involved in reading
- improve comprehension and retention (Roe and Smith 2005, 95)

Generally, there are several purposes for reading science texts:

- to learn something new or deepen knowledge
- to gather information for research and writing
- to answer a question

- to entertain/enjoy
- to follow instructions or perform steps in an experiment
- to confirm or reject a prediction
- to learn about a writer's craft (e.g., text organization/ structure or an author's writing style)

Teachers can advance students' understanding of specific science texts by making the purposes for reading explicit and clear. For example, the purposes for reading the engaging book, *Jess Makes Hair Gel* by Jacqueline Barber (2007) include learning to:

- think like a scientist
- design a mixture
- deepen scientific literacy skills, including literal, inferential, and critical/creative reading comprehension
- write about science, using science vocabulary and concepts
- follow instructions to engage in hands-on science activities, demonstrations, or experiments

Students should also be encouraged to *develop their own purposes* for reading by developing their own questions, which creates excitement about learning science. Encourage students to pose their own questions—just like Galileo did over 400 years ago and scientists do today. New research shows that making this single change in teaching has a positive impact on engaging students in reading and learning (Rothstein and Santana 2011).

To support students in creating questions that help them set a purpose for reading, guide them to review the following:

- the title
- the pictures, charts, or diagrams
- the bold headings

Students can then create questions that they want to learn about based on what they find in those features of the text. After they devise their preview questions, the teacher can remind them that they will soon read with the purpose of discovering answers to their own questions. This technique works well because students are often more engaged and motivated to read when they themselves create some of the questions. Questions that students might ask about *Jess Makes Hair Gel* could include:

- What is hair gel?
- Why does Jess want to make hair gel?
- How does Jess make hair gel?
- What is a mixture?

Building Students' Science Vocabulary

Catherine Snow (2010, 2002) and her colleagues (Snow, Lawrence, and White 2009) and Nonie Lesaux (2013) have found that a key to closing the achievement gap between advantaged and less advantaged students lies in teaching general academic vocabulary and the domain-specific vocabulary essential for learning a particular content area—in this case, science. Lesaux (2013) also explains that students need multiple experiences with new science vocabulary in order to understand concepts deeply. Therefore, before students read a science text, it's helpful for teachers to select and pre-teach unfamiliar science vocabulary words that are important for understanding the science concepts.

Teachers can write the new words on the board and pre-teach them in a meaningful context, using phrases and sentences directly from the book. An alternative is for the teacher to create new sentences. Teaching vocabulary in a meaningful context in this way enables students to develop a deeper understanding of word meanings. In contrast, learning lists of single, isolated words results in superficial learning and is less effective. Figure 3.1 presents four steps for systematically teaching science vocabulary. This vocabulary approach requires presenting new words in meaningful sentences, rather than in isolation. With practice, students become familiar with this routine, internalize it, and eventually do it on their own.

Teachers can apply this same approach to the science vocabulary in any book. To do this, the teacher selects and copies the words in context from sentences as they appear in the science book they are using. An alternative is for teachers to create their own meaningful sentences using new science words from a science text the class is using.

Figure 3.1 Four Steps for Pre-Teaching Science Vocabulary

1. The teacher and students read each sentence aloud and think about the meaning of the selected new vocabulary word.

2. Students guess possible meanings of the new science vocabulary, using the context and background knowledge of words and word parts.

3. The teacher encourages students' guesses about new word meanings and encourages students to explain their rationales; then the teacher provides feedback about the actual word meanings.

4. **Optional:** Students check the precise meaning in the book's glossary or in an online or print dictionary.

Based on these four steps, here are examples of vocabulary in context from sentences in *Jess Makes Hair Gel*:

- Jess decided to make *hair gel* because he wanted his hair to look *shiny* and *spiky*.
- Jess *wondered* what *ingredients* to use.
- Jess *recorded* what he learned by making a *table* in his notebook.
- Jess wrote down the word *substances*—a word *scientists* use for ingredients.
- Jess *compared* many substances. He used a *mixture* of gelatin *powder* and water and put the *mixture* in the microwave.
- Jess observed the gelatin *dissolve* in the water.
- Jess learned that *property* is a science word that means something you can see, smell, hear, feel, or taste about an ingredient.

Science vocabulary games provide multisensory experiences and multiple exposures to words necessary for deep understanding and recall. Here are two engaging science vocabulary games, which should be played after introducing and explaining each word's meaning in context.

Total Physical Response (TPR)

1. The teacher displays the selected vocabulary words.

2. As a class, the teacher and students decide on an action for each of the displayed vocabulary words (e.g., roots = point fingers toward the floor, wiggle fingers, and move hands toward the floor like roots growing into the ground).

3. Once all of the vocabulary words have a designated action, the students play "Simon Says"; the teacher calls out a word and students perform the action associated with that word's meaning.

Sharing Science

1. The teacher displays the vocabulary words from the lesson or unit and gives each student three to four counters/markers.

2. The students are placed into groups of three to five.

3. The teacher explains the following rules:
   - Every time a student says a sentence with one of the vocabulary words in it, he or she gives away a counter.

   - The sentences must supply a definition or present the word in a meaningful context. (Strong example = Humans need *oxygen* to breathe. Weak example = I like *water.*)

   - The students have to give away all of their counters.

   - Once a student's counters are "spent," he or she is not allowed to say anything anymore.

   - Students must be respectful and listen to the vocabulary sentences from all of their group mates.

4. Students generate sentences using the displayed vocabulary until all students have "spent" their counters.

Asking Rich 3-Leveled Comprehension Questions

To spur critical thinking during and after reading science texts, it's extremely important to include all three of the following levels of comprehension questions:

- lower-level factual questions
- higher-level inferential questions
- higher-level open-ended, critical-/creative-thinking questions.

Including all three levels of questions and teaching students to support their answers with textual evidence helps students meet state and national standards that emphasize textual evidence and analysis. To teach students to use text-based evidence, the teacher guides them to justify their answers by underlining or putting sticky notes on the places in the text where they found the answers. In the case of inferential or open-ended questions, students place a sticky note or underline the words in the text that supply a clue to the answer or support their reasoning.

Depending on the students' needs, the teacher can demonstrate marking inferential evidence by pointing out examples in the text before students attempt this task independently.

This three-level questioning technique can be used with any text. Examples of the three levels of questions for *Jess Makes Hair Gel* are:

1. **Factual/literal question:** What properties of good hair gel did Jess put on his list?

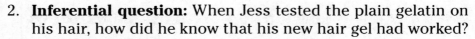

2. **Inferential question:** When Jess tested the plain gelatin on his hair, how did he know that his new hair gel had worked?

3. **Open-ended, critical-/creative-thinking questions:**
   - What do you think the properties of toothpaste might be?
   - How could you investigate to discover the properties of toothpaste?
   - How do you think scientists can help make our lives better?
   - Would you like to be a scientist and discover new things? Why?
   - What things would you like to investigate? Why?
   - What questions would you like to ask a scientist?

Fascinating science questions can spur curiosity and serve as a springboard for introducing a new science topic. For example, climate change is one of the salient issues of the 21st century. To introduce a unit on climate change, teachers might pose the following questions:

- What do we already know about climate change?
- What are the ecological impacts of climate change?
- What does the future hold regarding climate change?
- What can we do about climate change?
- Can we slow the process of climate change? If so, how?
- Can we halt climate change completely? Why?

(Adapted from Johnson 2009)

Using the 3-2-1 Method for Informational Texts

Nell Duke emphasizes the importance of reading informational texts, beginning in the earliest grades and continuing throughout the school years (Duke 2013, 2007; Duke et al. 2011). One effective way to promote excitement about informational texts and improve scientific literacy is by using The 3-2-1 Method (Duke 2013). The collaborative nature of this approach increases comprehension and retention of science concepts while providing practice in reading, speaking, listening, and questioning. This method is a terrific way to enhance students' scientific learning and meet Next Generation Science and literacy goals simultaneously.

The 3-2-1 Method

With The 3-2-1 Method, students read a science text and then engage in a Turn and Talk session. This involves pairs of students turning to each other and talking about the following:

- 3 things that they discovered from the reading

- 2 things that they found interesting about the reading

- 1 question that they still have about the reading

The 3-2-1 Method is easy to implement as a whole-class activity; students remain in their seats and simply turn and talk to the person sitting nearby.

Encourage older students to write first; then have them turn and talk to a partner about what they wrote.

Teaching Scientific Literacy through Writing

Next Generation Science Standards emphasize hands-on experimentation, which promotes students' scientific interests and propels their learning. In my interviews with famous scientists, including a Nobel laureate and other major prizewinners, I discovered that they had immersed themselves in hands-on science activities, beginning as early as elementary school. Without their ability to write and record information about their experiments, their learning would have been extremely limited. Teachers should provide rich science writing experiences to ensure thoughtful learning and deep comprehension of science concepts. Current literacy standards emphasize rich writing experiences in various genres, including science.

To address these standards and make science come alive, the teacher can integrate interesting and challenging activities after students read a science text or conduct an experiment. The following activities simultaneously support scientific inquiry and literacy learning, and they're a lot of fun.

Writing Activities in Science

- Write a letter to a scientist. Ask the scientist about the work being done in his or her laboratory.

- Visit a science laboratory. To arrange a visit, locate a scientist by contacting the science department of a local college, university, science center, or pharmaceutical company. It's beneficial for teachers to help students compile questions ahead of time and to encourage them to learn about the lab in advance from books or the Internet. Afterwards, have students conduct a follow-up writing activity, art activity, or scientific demonstration related to their laboratory experience to cement their learning.

- Write an original, student-created Reader's Theater script about a science text. (Alternatively, the teacher can write the script.) Have students perform the Reader's Theater script for another group, class, school assembly, or parent meeting.

- Publish or display the students' written work about any aspect of the science text or experiment in several venues—the classroom, school hallway, school magazine, school website, or a class book.

Science Verse, written by Jon Scieszka and illustrated by Lane Smith, contains zany, quirky, hilarious poems about wide-ranging science topics, such as black holes, the food chain, planets and the solar system, dinosaurs, the human body, the states of matter, atoms, protons, quarks, and electrons. Each poem is set to the rhythm and tune of a traditional song or poem, making it easy for students to learn the tune and rhythm while they learn new scientific information.

Scientific inquiry entails learning about domain-specific vocabulary, scientific concepts, logical reasoning, methods of observation, and different types of scientific evidence. After being introduced to the components of the scientific process, students can review the components by learning the "Scientists Use Observation Rap" shown in Appendix B. In order to help students synthesize information about the scientific process, teachers can combine science and English activities by having students write about the scientific process. Guiding students in writing a clearly developed paragraph on a science topic helps them simultaneously meet Next Generation Science Standards and literacy goals. Teachers can provide the following prompt and guidelines:

Write a well-developed paragraph in which you identify and explain each aspect of the scientific process. Your paragraph should include the following components as they relate to the scientific process.

- **Topic Sentence**—Is the prompt restated into a topic sentence that introduces the paragraph? Is the main idea clear?

- **Supporting Details**—Does each detail support or tell more about the topic?

- **Logical Order**—Does the order of the supporting details make sense? Does the order follow the scientific process from beginning to end?

- **Transitions** (or linking words)—Do linking words, or transitional phrases, connect details so that the paragraph reads smoothly?

- **Conclusion**—Does the conclusion restate the topic in a new way or tie the details together effectively?

- **Grammar and Mechanics**—Does the paragraph demonstrate command of the rules of spelling, grammar, and mechanics of writing?

- **Science Vocabulary**—Does the paragraph use science vocabulary terms and depict the scientific process clearly and effectively?

Scientific Writing and Research

Teaching Scientific Writing

Writing is a powerful tool to cement learning and assess conceptual understanding. However, writing is often challenging for students. Capitalizing on students' natural wonder creates an enticing bridge from conceptual learning to written demonstration. One possible topic likely to interest students is a unit about astronauts and the United States' program of manned missions to Mars. After students read online and print texts about the US Space Program, they can engage in research, writing, debates, and other forms of inquiry to explore various opinions or arguments in favor of and opposed to the manned missions to Mars. The teacher can suggest that students consider a variety of perspectives and opinions. After introducing each perspective, guide students to select the statement that best reflects their own opinions; then encourage them to write an opinion or argument supporting their points of view. Here are suggestions for teaching:

1. Select the statement with which you agree from the following options:

   - Manned missions to Mars are worth the cost, time, and risks involved.

   - Manned missions to Mars are not worth the cost, time, and risks involved.

   - There are many ways for the United States to reduce the cost of manned missions to Mars.

   - The United States gained a significant amount of valuable knowledge from our lunar program.

2. Write an essay supporting your point of view.

3. Include as many convincing details as possible.

Specific writing guidelines help students write more convincing opinion/argument essays. Some suggested guidelines are:

1. Introduce the topic and clearly state the main ideas of your argument.

2. Include strong claims to support your argument.

3. Link your claims and your argument together with specific transitional words and phrases.

4. Support your claims with relevant textual evidence from print, online, or multimedia sources.

5. Briefly acknowledge a counterargument.

6. End with a concluding statement or paragraph that clearly and succinctly relates to your main idea.

Writing is also a great way for students to review and synthesize complex scientific information. By writing culminating essays that tie together a large body of information, students learn to synthesize information and consider it deeply. They reflect on the significance of scientific information and learn how disparate facts and details fit together into a bigger picture. This is the essence of synthesis, one of the most challenging, highest–level literacy and scientific skills to develop.

Encouraging Scientific Research

Encouraging scientific research in school motivates students and inspires them to appreciate the joys of science. At the same time, it enables them to meet Next Generation Science Standards as well as state and national literacy goals in reading, research, writing, and oral presentation skills. The teacher doesn't need to be a science expert to encourage students to do research and pursue their scientific interests. All that is needed is a desire to try something different and explore unique, hands-on activities.

- *Sports Science: 40 Goal-Scoring, High-Flying, Medal-Winning Experiments for Kids!* by Jim Wiese (2002) contains intriguing sports-related experiments that engage students regardless of their skill level. Each experiment includes a list of simple materials, step-by-step procedures, and a concise explanation of the experiment's results. Thought–provoking questions that guide critical thinking and interpretation of each experiment are also included.

- *Teaching the Fun of Science* by Janice VanCleave (2001) makes the scientific process fun with its focus on intriguing topics, such as your weight on different planets and static electricity.

- *Think It, Show It Science: Strategies for Demonstrating Knowledge* by Gregory A. Denman (2013) emphasizes writing as a way to help students demonstrate their knowledge of science concepts. The varied activities in this book are accompanied by explicit instructions, making it easy for teachers to follow.

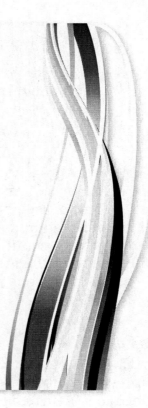

After introducing a science research topic and pre-teaching key vocabulary, teachers can encourage students to write or tell a partner four questions they have about the topic. For example, after reading Melissa Stewart's (2006) enticing book *A Place for Butterflies*, some questions students may wonder about when they do research on butterflies are:

- Why do butterflies appeal to us?

- What is most fascinating about butterflies?

- Where do female butterflies lay their eggs?

- Why are some kinds of butterflies having difficulty surviving today?

- What can people do to help butterflies thrive and grow?

These questions can become the driving force behind students' research on butterflies. The Internet is a fabulous resource for information, but Internet research projects present teachers with a unique 21st century caveat: not all websites are created equal. Students need to be taught not only the mechanics of conducting Internet searches, but also how to evaluate the quality and credibility of Internet information. By teaching students to evaluate websites and other Internet sources and giving students hands-on practice using these skills, teachers help them meet the important digital research goals of state and national standards.

Resources to Support Teaching with the Internet

- *CyberKids: Struggling Readers and Writers and How Computers Can Help* (Wood 2014)
- "Guiding Principles for Supporting New Literacies in Your Classroom" (Karchmer-Klein and Shinas 2012).
- *Literacy Online: New Tools for Struggling Readers and Writers* (Wood 2004).
- *Teaching with the Internet K–12: New Literacies for New Times* (Leu, Leu, and Coiro 2004).

We need to teach students explicitly that some websites are more accurate and reliable than others. One way to teach students to distinguish truth from falsehood on the Internet is to teach them to evaluate websites according to five key areas: authority, responsibility, currency, point of view, and purpose (Adapted from Lesley University Library 2014).

1. **Authority**—the person or group responsible for the website's information

   • Who created the website?

   • Can you find any credentials or qualifications? What are they?

   • If the website was created by an organization, what is the reputation of the organization?

   • Is there a way to contact the author? How?

2. **Responsibility**—indication of the source of the information

   • Where did the information come from? Is there a way to indicate the origin of the information, such as a formal bibliography, works cited, or reference list?

   • Who decides on the content of the website? Is it an individual, an organization, or a formal editorial board?

   • What credentials are provided, such as expertise, education, and/or experience?

3. **Currency**—indication of how recent or up-to-date the information is

   • Can you find a publication or creation date? What is it?

   • Does the topic require very current information? Why?

   • If there is a bibliography or reference list, are the dates of those sources within the last ten years?

   • Are there some "oldies but goodies" in the references, that is, older sources that still contain useful and important information? How can you tell?

4. **Point of View**—a particular way of thinking

   • Can you detect a bias or strong point of view in the information? How?

- If there is a bias, do the authors acknowledge their point of view by stating it up front?

- Does the information include or acknowledge more than one point of view on the topic? Does it acknowledge other viewpoints in a respectful manner even when disagreeing?

5. **Purpose**—the reason for presenting the information

- What is the author's purpose? Can you readily discern the purpose?

- Is the primary purpose to:
  ➤ educate and inform?
  ➤ persuade?
  ➤ sell a product? (Note: a good rule of thumb while doing research projects is to avoid using information whose purpose is to sell something.)

- Is the information detailed and thorough, or does the information seem short and superficial, skimming the surface, and lacking in depth?

Rapping and Singing about Science

Rapping and singing are enticing ways to review scientific facts and concepts. Students can compose their own raps about scientific topics they're studying, such as butterflies, the environment, climate change, plate tectonics, and the solar system. Or, they can sing and perform the science songs in this book, such as "Butterflies Are Beautiful" (to the tune of "Mary Had a Little Lamb") shown next. This song summarizes information about monarch butterflies based on Melissa Stewart's engaging book *A Place for Butterflies* (2006). Singing is a great way for students to review what they learn about monarchs, a popular butterfly species that lives throughout the United States as well as in Canada and Mexico.

Butterflies Are Beautiful

by Rosalie Fink

(Sung to the tune of "Mary Had A Little Lamb")

Chorus

Butterflies are beautiful,
Colorful and beautiful.
Butterflies are beautiful
And they're graceful too.

We love the way they flutter by
The butterflies just flutter by.
We love the way they flutter by
And land on flowers too.

Verse 1

Monarchs always lay their eggs
On milkweed plants, milkweed plants
'Cause that's the only food that monarch
Caterpillars eat.

Verse 2

But milkweed makes the cattle sick
It makes them sick, makes them sick.
It gives the cows a bellyache
So farmers kill milkweed.

Verse 3

Farmers might let milkweed grow
Milkweed grow, milkweed grow
Farmers might let milkweed grow,
Where cattle do not graze.

Verse 4

Then butterflies will live and thrive,
Live and thrive, live and thrive,
Then butterflies will live and thrive.
Their species will survive.

Chorus

Another example of how to incorporate rhythm and rap into science lessons is through Steve Sheinkin's (2012) award-winning book *Bomb: The Race to Build—and Steal—the World's Most Dangerous Weapon*. This fascinating book reads like a fast-paced mystery and reveals the suspenseful competition of the race to make the first atomic bomb. In retelling this captivating true story about the discovery of uranium and how scientists from different countries competed, *Bomb* shows how science discoveries and inventions relate to national and international politics and affect our lives. The intriguing spy story in *Bomb* makes the book a real page-turner. Students simultaneously learn about uranium, radioactivity, and fission while learning about the history of World War II.

After students read about the elements, teachers can help reinforce the scientific facts by having students write summaries that capture the key points, or by writing their own raps about an element of their choice. For example, sixth-grade teacher Ms. Jones told each student in her Newton, Massachusetts class to write an original rap about an element of interest. Each rap had to summarize basic facts about the element, since the purpose of the rap was to help students review for an upcoming science test. Below is an original rap about the element uranium, written by student Ben Feldman, now in sixth grade and still using rhythm and rap to further his studies.

The Uranium Rap

by Ben Feldman
(Sung to the tune of "Party Rock Anthem" by LMFAO)

Chorus
Party bomb is in the nuclear plants tonight.
They're made with uranium
Yeah, that's right.
And it gonna make you feel
So not right.
We just wanna see ya get your facts right.

First Verse

Uranium, I got to know
The melting point is 2070 Fahrenheit
Yo, I'm so caught up in this information
I be looking at the flow
Party bomb, ya, that the crew I rep
With no lead in our element, hey!

Chorus

Second Verse

Stop atomic numbas 92
Mo solid for us another one,
Boiling point is 7458 degrees
That's very great
We just wanna see
What's the atomic symbol gonna be
It's U now.
Martin Heinrich Klaproth discovered uranium.
Marie Curie figured out how to use it.
Uranium! Uranium! Uranium!

Chorus

Final Refrain (two times)

Every day we shouldn't be dropping bombs.
Uranium! Uranium! Uranium!

Drawing with Videos

Drawing is another powerful way to learn science, because it gives students the opportunity to visualize sizes, shapes, motions, and spatial relationships. An innovative approach called Draw-with-Me (King and King 2015) has students simultaneously watch a video and draw a scientific diagram. This multisensory approach to learning science simultaneously engages students in listening, observing, and drawing what they see, while meeting Next Generation Science goals for mastering complex Earth science vocabulary and concepts. It's an engaging way to present Earth science information about the spatial and movement aspects of plate tectonics (King and King 2015). Students can annotate their drawings by adding important facts and details about the Earth's crust, plate tectonics, and volcanoes. Then, they can use their drawings for reference, study-review sessions, report writing, and oral presentations.

In teaching this kind of lesson, the teacher can draw the illustrations side-by-side with students or, when time is short, present pre-drawn illustrations on a computer screen and annotate the illustrations while presenting the material. This method works best if students have their own pre-drawn illustrations to annotate. To access illustrations free of charge, visit www.geology.com/nsta.

Using Body Movement

Teaching through body movement is an extremely powerful multisensory approach (Jensen 2005). Teaching with body movement capitalizes on the brain's ability to use multisensory input to enhance learning (Murray 2015). For example, learning complex concepts in biology is greatly enhanced when the teacher integrates physical movement with science instruction. In her science classes, Alison Ament integrates a playful movement activity for teaching a basic neurology concept (Ament 2013). Ament uses the analogy of *the wave* to teach about nerve impulse transmission. The notion of the wave is familiar to many people, especially sports fans. The wave occurs when lots of people lift their arms one-by-one sequentially in a line around the stands at a sporting event. Similarly, nerve impulses pass along nerves in a predictable point-to-point manner. The sequential movement of sodium ions inward through the nerve cell membrane along the nerve constitutes the impulse. Students can use the familiar ballpark image to understand the similar sequential process in nerve impulse transmission. Steps for using body movements to demonstrate how nerves transmit impulses in the human body are as follows:

1. Have students sit or stand in a line around the room. (Each student represents a tiny portion of the nerve cell membrane.)

2. Give each student a paper plate with Na+ (the symbol for a sodium ion) written on it.

3. As the wave begins, the first student raises the Na+ paper plate overhead.

4. The next student takes the cue from the first student, and raises their paper plate overhead, and so on, thus modeling the stimulation of each part of the nerve cell from the segment before it. This continues until all students have raised a paper plate over their heads.

5. Then, each student lowers the Na+ paper plate, showing how the recovery wave follows closely upon the impulse wave. This means that each student raises a paper plate over his or her head and, immediately thereafter, lowers the paper plate. The result is an undulating wave-like motion, demonstrating the ongoing manner in which nerve impulses move and are transmitted in the human body.

Using this wave analogy is a very effective teaching strategy. The kinesthetic input from the physical body movements provides powerful imprinting on the brain, helping students understand and remember how nerves transmit impulses.

Conclusion

The popularity of science in the 21st century creates exciting opportunities to deepen students' scientific understanding and build on their natural curiosity. By integrating reading, writing, singing, drawing, rapping, and body movement with a variety of science activities, teachers add a novel dimension to science that reinforces and enriches traditional approaches. Innovative use of the arts and hands-on activities inspires excitement about scientific discoveries, conveys deep understanding of scientific concepts, and enables reinforcement and mastery of science vocabulary and knowledge. By sparking science lessons with captivating questions, engaging materials, and enticing activities, teachers can reach students of diverse backgrounds and abilities and enable all types of students to succeed in science.

Reflect and Discuss

1. What activities or strategies stood out most to you? Why?

2. What strategies, materials, and activities would you like to use in your science lessons? What challenges do you anticipate, and how would you address them?

3. How do you think the approaches in this chapter could help your students meet state and national goals for developing scientific knowledge and literacy skills?

4. Think about an upcoming science unit. How can you incorporate movement and rap strategically into that unit?

Chapter 4

Reading, Writing, and Rhythm in Social Studies

Questions to Activate Thinking

1. What is most rewarding and interesting for you about teaching social studies?

2. What challenges do you face in teaching social studies today?

3. What role does literacy development play in your social studies instruction?

4. How could you incorporate body movement into your social studies activities?

21st Century Social Studies Instruction

Social studies and literacy learning go hand-in-hand and can be taught together seamlessly, especially when teachers integrate literacy and the arts into their social studies lessons. This chapter features innovative social studies activities and resources that include rhythm, rap, song, drama, visual arts, and hands-on activities designed to ignite students' curiosity and enthusiasm for social studies. Each activity is designed to help history and social studies come alive. The activities are aligned with state and national standards to address specific skills in social studies reading, writing, speaking, listening, language, media, and technology.

Teaching social studies today means covering a broad range of topics and time frames, from ancient Greek and Roman civilizations to life in 21st century America and the global community. Current social studies standards include not only learning about historical facts, concepts, and controversies, but also learning about how history may differ, depending on the perspective of the historical writer. To meet rigorous new standards, social studies teachers must communicate major historical themes and details as well as the process of how history is understood from different historical perspectives. Teachers also need to convey to students that, as American citizens, they have an important participatory role in shaping our nation and the world. Teachers can help students meet the unique goals and exciting challenges of 21st century social studies curriculum by using music, rhythm, rap, drama, poetry, painting, and sculpture (Brice-Heath 1999; Editorial 2014; Paquette and Rieg 2008; Perret and Fox 2006).

Reading Inspiring Biographies

Reading inspiring biographies is an effective way for students to meet state and national standards in social studies reading, writing, speaking, listening, and research skills (Duke 2013, 2007). Biographies are especially well suited for teaching social studies when used alongside textbooks and Internet resources. Regardless of students' ages, biographies about inspiring heroes have wide appeal, and great, well-written biographies are irresistible for many students, including reluctant readers (Fink 2006, 1998, 1996). A good biography bridges the gap between narratives and informational texts because it simultaneously informs and tells an intriguing story.

Today, biographies are highly recommended for students of all ages, including kindergarten and first graders, because recent research shows that students who read informational texts early (such as biographies) are more likely to succeed later in life than students who lack these crucial experiences (Duke 2013, 2007 Duke et al. 2011; National Institute of Child Health and Human Development 2000).

Teachers can choose from a list of inspiring biographies in the Social Studies section of Appendix C.

A wide variety of literacy activities can be used with biographies. For example:

Biography Activities

1. Use photographs of the person engaged in activities at various stages of his or her life as a springboard for discussion and writing about the person's personal and professional life.

2. Introduce vocabulary within the context of the book.

Biography Activities *(cont.)*

3. Ask reading comprehension questions to generate interest, background information, discussion, and writing. For example, ask:

- Where is the table of contents? Read it.

- What did you learn from reading the table of contents?

- What do you want to learn more about after reading the table of contents? Why?

- Where is the index of the book? What does the index tell you about where to find out about _____?

- Look at the photograph of _____ on page _____. (Ask a follow-up question that has students analyze the feelings of the person or the actions taking place in the image.)

- Look at the picture of _____. on page _____. Who are the people in the photograph? What does the caption say? (Ask a follow-up question that has students analyze the actions taking place or the event being described and its importance in the person's life.)

- Look at the picture on page _____, and read what it says on page _____. Compare what you learned from the picture and the text.

Biography Activities *(cont.)*

- Read page _____. Use the Internet to find out more about _____. What are some key words you will use to search for information on the Internet? Why did you choose these search words?

- After reading this book, what did you learn and what did you find most interesting? Explain. What else would you like to learn about?

There are lots of fascinating biographies that are appropriate for K–12 classrooms. Two examples about US presidents are: *If I Were President* by Catherine Stier (2004), for grades 2–5, and *The Book of the Presidents: With Portraits by Distinguished American Artists* by Vincent Wilson, Jr. (2013), for secondary grades. Some interesting activities for students to engage in before, during, and after reading either of these books (or others) are:

Before Reading

- Ask questions, such as: What does the president of The United States do and what are some of the responsibilities that come with the job of leading our country?

- Lead a discussion based on responses from the class.

- Based on the discussion, generate a list of the president's responsibilities.

During Reading

Set specific purposes for reading and share them with the class. Specific purpose-setting helps focus students' attention and enhance their understanding and memory of text information. For example, the teacher might direct students to do the following:

- read to find out how a person becomes president

- read to find out what the president's jobs and responsibilities are

- read to find out what it's like to live in the White House

- read to find out about the pets and children who lived in the White House in the past and today

After Reading

Extend learning by having students complete tasks such as:

Create a catchy campaign slogan, and design a bumper sticker on a 4" × 10" piece of construction paper. Display the bumper stickers in your class.

Work with a partner and create a two-, three-, or four-line song, rap, or poem that includes the campaign slogan. Perform your campaign rap, song, or poem for the class, using clapping or hand or body movement to the rhythm.

Many presidents bring their pets to the White House. For example, President Obama brought his Portuguese water dog, Bo; President Johnson brought his beagles, Him and Her; and President Kennedy brought his daughter's pony, Macaroni. Have students write about and illustrate a pet using the following ideas:

1. Imagine that you are the first family's pet. What kind of animal would you be?

2. Describe a day in your life as a pet at the White House. Use three specific details about your experiences there. (e.g., Will you sit underneath the president's desk while the president signs bills into law or meets with world leaders? What might you hear the president or others saying? Will you beg for food during fancy dinners with world leaders and politicians?)

3. Draw, paint, or sculpt the pet you described in writing; then display your written description and artwork in the classroom, in a school display case, on a bulletin board, or website.

4. Create a rhythmic rap, jingle, or poem about your pet and recite it for a school assembly or event to which another class or family and friends are invited.

Make a T-chart comparing the pros and cons of being president. Which parts of the president's job do you think would be enjoyable for you? Which parts of the job would be challenging for you? Compare your T-chart with a partner's T-chart. Discuss how they are similar and different.

The president's job is to identify problems in our country and find solutions to these problems. Prompt students to do the following:

1. Look around the classroom, school, or neighborhood, and observe problems that exist around them. (e.g., Is there too much trash scattered around the cafeteria? Are there too few balls for playing at recess?) Have students identify a problem that matters to them.

2. Have students meet with their "cabinet" (a small group of classmates) to generate a possible solution to the problem and write down their group's ideas.

3. Encourage each group to poll students in the class or school about the problem and whether they agree or disagree with the proposed solution. Then, have them present their findings to the class, the principal, the teacher, or the school's student council.

4. Have students write an article for the school newspaper or school website in support of their solution, or draw a picture of the problem before and after their solution. Then exhibit the picture on a school bulletin board or website. Students could also create a rhythmic rap or short song to support their solution to the problem. They could then perform it at a school assembly or for a local radio station.

Many lesser-known individuals throughout American history have made significant contributions, and it's important to teach about them for two reasons. First, the contributions of women and people of color to our country were almost entirely overlooked in American history prior to the 1960s civil rights movement. Subsequently, many new faces have been included in American history books; however, a few luminaries, such as Booker T. Washington and Martin Luther King, Jr., often overshadow the contributions of lesser-known figures. A second reason is that students identify more readily with less famous individuals, since they often do not see themselves as outstanding and famous. Here's a suggestion for creating an activity about lesser-known historical figures:

1. The teacher pre-selects a list of choices and students choose individuals from the list, such as Frederick McKinley Jones (inventor of refrigeration systems used on trucks that deliver food) and Cathay Williams (first black woman to enlist and serve in the US Army).

2. Students conduct research about a lesser-known person of interest to them.

3. Students then write short summaries highlighting the contributions of their selected individual.

4. Each student then uses the summary to create a page that outlines important facts about the individual.

5. Students include photographs, drawings, or other visual aids for their pages.

6. Students create their own paintings, poems, songs, or raps about the individual and add these original works to their pages.

7. The teacher creates a class book composed of each student's page about the individual.

8. Then, the teacher poses a question for discussion: What effects do you think these men and women have had on your life and the life of your family?

9. Students engage in a writing activity in response to the questions.

10. Students share their responses with a partner, small group, or the whole class.

11. As a culminating activity, display the book in a prominent public area, such as the front entrance of the school or the school website.

(Adapted from Stier 2004)

Researching and Writing about Biographies

Guiding students to write clear, concise summaries about an individual's life from dense expository texts helps them deepen their understanding and increase their retention of complex social studies concepts, vocabulary, and facts. However, simply assigning summaries is not enough. Students need explicit, direct instruction about how to write without plagiarizing. The ability to summarize a text while avoiding plagiarism is an extremely important skill. It prepares students for future writing in high school, college, and the workplace. Teachers should provide specific guidance and practice in summary writing. They can guide students in the process and components of writing summaries by suggesting that students do the following:

Plagiarism is the act of presenting information you learned from a text as if it were your own original discovery without giving recognition to the original author. Plagiarism is considered theft—stealing somebody else's ideas. To avoid plagiarism, be sure to give credit to the author by citing the author appropriately.

1. State the main idea(s) in a clear topic sentence at the beginning of each paragraph.

2. In your own words and style, include important supporting facts and details in each paragraph based on the source you used.

3. Cite the source of your information and paraphrase what you learned in your own words as much as possible. Do not copy verbatim from the text you read.

To paraphrase:

- First, read your source carefully.
- Underline or place sticky notes beside facts and details that seem important.
- Then, look away from the text.
- Without looking, write down what you remember from the text in your own words.
- Now check back with the text to make sure that your facts are accurate.

4. Reread what you wrote, and using your judgment, omit the less important details.

5. Chunk similar ideas together.

6. Include a conclusion that restates the main idea and ties your whole summary together.

Using Music to Teach Social Studies

Music and singing provide an effective medium for students to experience social studies concepts on a deeper and more visceral level (Booth 2009). Not only is it fun and energizing, but music, rhythm, and song provide natural, engaging ways to deepen learning—ways that date far back in history (Seeger 2004; Sitomer and Cirelli 2004). Recent research suggests that using multisensory methods such as music, rhythm, and song improves learning outcomes (Murray 2015; Editorial 2014; Paquette and Rieg 2008; Perret and Fox 2006).

Teachers can use music to help students understand the social and historical contexts of historical periods and experience the emotions of bygone eras more deeply. A single well-chosen song or book that incorporates music can be both informative and inspiring. For example, *When Marian Sang: The True Recital of Marian Anderson, Voice of a Century* by Pam Muñoz Ryan (2002) tells the moving life story of the great African American opera singer Marian Anderson. This beautifully illustrated biography provides a foundation for lessons about many topics in the curriculum: American history, women's history, African American history, and music history. It dramatically narrates the gripping journey of Marian Anderson's life through story, song, and illustration. Song lyrics are interspersed throughout the text, which has the powerful effect of deepening the emotional impact of the dramatic events in Marian Anderson's life. The book includes the words, chords, and notes to each song, making it easy for teachers and students to sing along and immerse themselves in the narrative. Some of the songs included are:

- "Let My People Go"
- "Sometimes I Feel Like a Motherless Child"
- "My Country 'Tis of Thee"
- "Nobody Knows the Trouble I've Seen"
- "He's Got the Whole World in His Hands"

When Marian Sang: The True Recital of Marian Anderson, Voice of a Century is rich not only in song but in extraordinary word choices that will enrich students' vocabularies while they learn about segregation and Jim Crow laws. This book is excellent for teaching vocabulary in meaningful contexts by discussing and explaining the context clues. Here are examples of important words in their context to teach from this outstanding book:

- When her father died, *tragedy* filled Marian's heart.

- Marian knew about *prejudice* because she had seen the trolley drive past her family as they stood on the corner waiting to ride.

- No matter what *humiliations* she *endured*, Marian sang from her heart with *dignity*.

- Marian was *offered* a *momentous invitation* to sing at the Lincoln Memorial.

Teachers can use other outstanding books as well to integrate songs about American history into the social studies curriculum. For example, *Rise Up Singing: The Group Singing Songbook* edited by Peter Blood and Annie Patterson (2004) is a superb choice. Teachers can use the song "We Shall Overcome" in this book to teach a unit on the 1960s civil rights movement. Prior to singing, engage students in a discussion about how singing this particular song in unison during peaceful demonstrations became a way to rally, unify, and energize a whole generation of Americans, who marched together peacefully in order to demand integrated schools, integrated restaurants, and voter registration access for *all* Americans, regardless of their race. Some specific questions for whole-class discussions are:

- What does it mean to "overcome" something?

- What were the black and white demonstrators of the 1960s civil rights movement trying to "overcome"?

- How do you think singing "We Shall Overcome" in unison helped the demonstrations for equality succeed?

- What was the role of music and song in this political movement?

- What did the civil rights movement of the 1960s achieve?

- What civil rights work remains to be done now and in the future?

- What songs are being sung and what slogans are being used today to rally Americans to improve civil rights for all Americans in the 21st century?

Following these discussions, the teacher can provide the words and melody of "We Shall Overcome," shown in Figure 4.1. Have students sing in unison, holding hands and swaying left to right to the rhythm, as protesters of the 1960s did and as protesters have also done today. Teachers can encourage students to add relevant new verses about current events and other challenges to civil rights for all people in the 21st century.

Figure 4.1 We Shall Overcome Lyrics

We shall overcome, we shall overcome,

We shall overcome some day.

O deep in my heart, I do believe

We shall overcome some day!

Creating and singing new verses shows students that the civil rights movement is not over but continues today. It helps students connect historical movements to the 21st century. It also teaches them to value the power of their right to demonstrate peacefully to make positive changes in order to make our country fair and safe for all people.

The teacher can guide students to write their own lyrics to the same rhythm and melody, individually or in small groups of 2–5 students. Then, they can practice singing their new verses and perform for the class or a school assembly.

After singing, encourage students to create a dance of their own using the rhythm of "We Shall Overcome." To encourage freedom of movement, the teacher can have students bring in scarves, hold them high up over their heads, and move their arms and scarves from side to side, up and down, and twirl with the scarf. Students can also create costumes with the scarves: head pieces, hats, shawls, or outfits connoting different people.

An additional piece to add to a unit on civil rights is the rap "My President" about Rosa Parks and President Barack Obama "running [for office] so we all can fly," which was composed by rap artist Jay-Z (2010). Teachers can use the rap lines from this song for historical and rhetorical analyses. A good way to help students meet state and national goals in social studies and literacy is by guiding them to analyze the complex, metaphorical language and rhetorical devices in this rap. Analyzing Jay-Z's nuanced words helps students understand this rapper's adept use of language and strong metaphors. In "My President," Jay-Z portrays the sweep of history from the 1960s civil rights movement to the present and into the future. The phrase "so we all can fly" suggests an unbounded future of a nation in which *all* Americans are free and feel wonderful—as if they are flying.

> *"Rosa Parks sat so Martin Luther King could walk. Martin Luther King walked so Obama could run. Obama's running so we all can fly."*
> —"My President" by Jay-Z (2010)

In explaining the complex meaning of Jay-Z's words, teachers can help students meet college and career readiness standards in social studies and literacy by guiding them to analyze, write, and give multimedia presentations about civil rights in America, past, present, and future. The following is a lesson example for middle school.

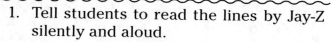

1. Tell students to read the lines by Jay-Z silently and aloud.

2. Ask: "How does Jay-Z use verbs in this part of the rap? How are the verbs *walk*, *run*, and *fly* used metaphorically to suggest different specific meanings based on what you know about history? Explain your answers by using facts and details you know."

3. Have students do individual text, video, and Internet research about Rosa Parks, Martin Luther King, Jr., and Barack Obama.

4. Guide students to use credible sources with multiple points of view.

5. After students read primary and secondary sources about the civil rights movement of the 1960s and the election of President Barack Obama in 2008 and 2012, have them revisit their initial discussion about the specific meanings in Jay-Z's words: *walk*, *run*, and *fly*.

6. Ask: "What have you learned by reading the primary and secondary sources you used? How has your understanding and knowledge deepened? Explain."

7. Prompt students to compare and contrast the various contributions of Rosa Parks, Martin Luther King, Jr., and Barack Obama by selecting from a list of options, such as:

    - drawing pictures
    - creating paintings
    - making sculptures
    - writing songs

8. Guide students to write well-developed expository essays comparing and contrasting the contributions of Rosa Parks, Martin Luther King, Jr., and Barack Obama.

9. Have students plan oral presentations based on their comparative essays and present what they learned to the class. Encourage the use of multimedia as adjuncts to their oral presentations.

10. Have students in the audience give constructive feedback to each speaker by using the guidelines provided in Figure 4.2. (See Appendix C for a full-size version.)

11. To review what they have learned, have students form small groups of 3–6 to create their own original rap or Reader's Theater script about Rosa Parks, Martin Luther King, Jr., Barack Obama, or any other individual or group relevant to the struggle for civil rights. These can be historical figures or people in the news who are working to expand civil rights and justice for all people today.

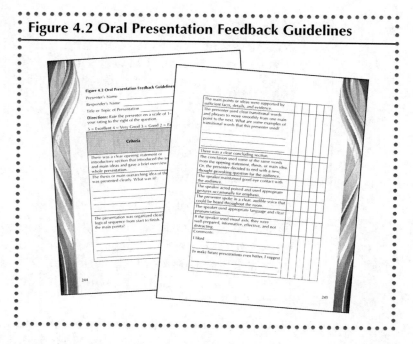

Figure 4.2 Oral Presentation Feedback Guidelines

There are many ways to link historical research with songs. Some additional activities that involve singing and research are as follows:

- Students studying colonial times and the founding of the United States can sing "America the Beautiful" and "This Land Is Your Land." They can then do grade-appropriate text and Internet research about topics relevant to themes in these songs.

- Students studying the Civil War or the civil rights movement can sing and then do text and Internet research projects that tie in with the following songs: "Harriet Tubman," "Black and White," "Birmingham Sunday," and "We Shall Overcome."

- After conducting research and writing their research papers, students can share what they learned by presenting their projects orally to a partner, the whole class, or the whole school in a school-wide assembly to which families and friends are invited. In addition to sharing their research projects, the class as a whole can perform a few of the songs for the assembly.

Using Multisensory Approaches

Recent research shows that learning is greatly enhanced when all of the senses are involved (Murray 2015). One way to involve the senses is to use drama to enhance instruction. Acting out stories and discussing them, followed by research and writing activities, helps students deepen their comprehension and remember what they've read (Rinne et al. 2011). The multisensory nature of these activities includes speaking, listening, moving, gesturing, and reflecting, all of which help form strong representations of information in the brain. This promotes deep comprehension and enhances memory and overall learning (Murray 2015; Rinne et al. 2011). To capitalize on the benefits of multisensory learning, teachers can use a variety of extension activities, including Reader's Theater, Freeze Frames, research writing, and oral presentations. The following are some examples:

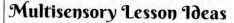

Multisensory Lesson Ideas

- Have students write, and then perform, a Reader's Theater script based on the text. (See Chapter 2 for Reader's Theater instructions.)

- Give students a choice of creating Reader's Theater scripts that reflect what actually happened or creating Reader's Theater scripts that change a key turning point in the actual story so that the result differs from the original text.

- Have students do a Freeze Frame enactment. (See the next section, Using Freeze Frames to Re-enact History, for specifics.)

- Have students conduct a comparison/contrast research project about a topic relevant to the text and present their findings to the class as an oral presentation that employs multimodal texts.

Using Freeze Frames to Re-enact History

Freeze Frames are a highly motivating form of drama in which students act out significant historical events while the audience plays guessing games about the unfolding drama. Evidence from neuroscientists and cognitive scientists reveals that Freeze Frames and other dramatic enactments are not only motivating and fun but have positive learning outcomes (Craik and Watkins 1973; Defeyter, Russo, and McPartlin 2009; Murray 2015; Rinne et al. 2011).

Luke Rinne and his colleagues have shown that translating text material into dramatic actions results in improved recall of information (Rinne et al. 2011). Since acting entails motor encoding, verbal encoding, and physical movement, the combined use of these multisensory inputs provides deeper processing, resulting in stronger memory in the brain. Rinne explains that the "unusualness" of the actions during drama also makes the information easier to remember (Rinne et al. 2011).

Freeze Frames are an effective technique to improve students' retention and deepen their understanding of complex historical events (Rasinski and Samuels 2011; Rinne et al. 2011; Wilhelm 2002). This dramatic approach depends on movement to help students deepen their understanding of complex social studies texts. Freeze Frames can be created by students in small groups and then shared with the whole class. Some good topics for using Freeze Frames are:

- the Pilgrims at Plymouth Rock
- the first Thanksgiving
- the Boston Tea Party
- the signing of the Declaration of Independence
- immigrants arriving at Ellis Island
- the assassination of President Abraham Lincoln
- passage of the 19th Amendment
- the building of the Great Wall of China
- the collapse of the Berlin Wall
- the burial of King Tut

The following are steps to implement Freeze Frames:

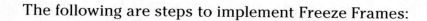

Freeze Frames

1. Form small groups of 3–6 students each.

2. Each group chooses a significant historical event from the text.

3. Each group plans how it will represent this event as a Freeze Frame action.

4. Each group chooses a role for each student in representing the historical event.

5. Each group presents its Freeze Frame to the class.

6. The teacher says, "One, two, freeze," at which time students hold their places and expressions and do not move.

7. The audience attempts to guess what historical episode or scene is being portrayed.

8. If necessary, members of the audience may say, "We need hints." Then, the teacher taps one student in the performing group. That student utters a line or makes a gesture that is characteristic of the historical figure.

9. The audience guesses who the historical figure is and what event the group on stage is representing.

Exploring Multiple Perspectives

New state and national standards emphasize the importance of understanding history and current events from multiple perspectives and identities. This is especially important in our nation of immigrants with its history of slavery, discrimination, and injustice—as well as its great opportunities for people from all over the world.

To help students understand the feelings of people who are different from them, teachers can provide opportunities to read, view, listen, think, write, and perform from multiple perspectives. One way to do this is to highlight commonalities and differences among groups of people by exploring texts and individuals with multiple perspectives about the same issue. Multiple perspectives can address differences in chronological time, geographical setting, race, gender, age, socioeconomic status, political philosophy, and ethnic and religious background.

Writing, singing, dancing, acting, and using visual arts can enhance students' knowledge and understanding of a variety of groups and cultures.

Another powerful way to explore multiple perspectives and identities is by having students create a specific identity based on a fictitious, yet realistic, individual. The teacher can explain that inequities still exist and discuss the historical origins of today's inequities. Perhaps most importantly, the teacher should explain that these inequities do not have to persist. Explain that students can take positive action in their own communities and their country to make important changes to end injustice, inequities, and unfairness based on race, gender, and socioeconomic class. The following activity guides students to create imaginary identities. The purpose of this absorbing activity is to help students consider experiences from multiple perspectives that differ from their own (Adapted from www. reading.org):

Multiple Perspectives

1. First, each student chooses an age, gender, race, and geographic location, such as a 12-year-old African American girl in Chicago; a 13-year-old Latino boy in New York City; a 10-year-old Caucasian girl in Charlotte, North Carolina; or a 21-year-old African American man in Boston.

2. The teacher presents prompts, such as:

   • What type of job/occupation, home, and family might this person have?

   • What political beliefs might this person have?

   (Note: It's important to discuss stereotypes with students to ensure that stereotypes are not perpetuated through this activity.)

3. Students research answers to the above questions for three different time periods (e.g., 1852, 1965, and 2015). The teacher provides sufficient time and guidance for conducting the research and guides students to notice how the social and political worlds of the imagined characters developed during the three different time periods.

4. After researching, students read, listen to, and/or watch three speeches that occurred during the selected time periods. (e.g., "The Meaning of July Fourth for a Negro" by Frederick Douglas—1852 [Foner 1950], "American Dream" by Martin Luther King, Jr.—August 28, 1963 [Rappaport 2001], and "Remarks by the President at Fourth of July Celebration" by Barack Obama—July 4, 2013 [Obama 2013])

5. Students choose how to have their characters respond to the speeches. Options can include:

   • write a letter to a newspaper editor stating the character's reaction to the speech
   • give a mock statement to the press
   • craft a tweet
   • create an Instagram post

6. Students then share their responses with a partner or a whole group.

Another engaging way to teach about the concept of multiple perspectives is to emphasize great American ideals and values, such as democracy, equity, and equality for all people. Teaching Tolerance provides outstanding free history lesson plans that do an excellent job of meeting these social studies goals (see www.teachingtolerance.org). The materials are easily adaptable for different ages and grade levels and can incorporate the strategies for integrating rhythm and the arts that are described throughout this book. Additional poems and raps on this topic, such as "Fairness for All," are provided in Appendix B.

Exploring Identity through Writing, Art, Genealogy, and Folktales

To teach the meaning of identity, it's helpful to have students reflect on their own evolving concepts of themselves. One way to do this is through descriptive writing and artwork. The teacher can explain that we each have "hybrid" identities that simultaneously include our gender, age, race, religion, and ethnicity. To begin, the teacher can share a personal experience in which his or her identity was challenged—an episode in which the teacher experienced prejudice and discrimination based on gender, race, ethnicity, religion, or socioeconomic class. The teacher's candid sharing of personal experiences of discrimination helps establish trust and openness about these sensitive topics.

Next, students write about their own identity experiences and create accompanying artwork. Afterwards, they read their papers and share their artwork with a partner. It's a good idea to tell students in advance that they will share their work with a partner. Writing, drawing, and sharing experiences that shaped their identity helps students understand, respect, and empathize with students from different backgrounds. I have used this activity in my own teaching, and students have told me that this identity writing activity was one of the most memorable, life-changing experiences they had in school. This kind of experience can affect students profoundly; it can lead to increased self-understanding and result in greater knowledge, understanding, and empathy toward people from different backgrounds.

Folktales are another effective way for students to explore identity—their own and that of others. Folktales provide a strong springboard for exploring the history and sociology of a wide variety of cultures that have contributed to the rich diversity of the United States. By using folk literature in the curriculum, teachers ascribe value to each student's language and culture, as well as to English. Captivating folktales from around the globe are easily accessible; Appendix C has excellent suggestions.

Genealogy is another absorbing way for students to explore their identity. Fortunately, many resources are available, such as *Climbing Your Family Tree: Online and Off-Line Genealogy for Kids* by Ira Wolfman (2002). This book is filled with intriguing facts and activities, including digital and hard copy texts and teaching materials. It contains links to various sites to help guide students doing oral histories of their families. To implement oral histories and family interviews, the teacher can guide students to:

1. Prepare their questions. (See lists at www.workman.com/familytree and select questions that are relevant.)

2. Interview various family members, both immediate and more distant if possible, about their family history.

3. Type up notes from the interviews and ask relatives who were interviewed to review them and make corrections or additions.

4. Write a thank-you note to each family member who was interviewed.

(Adapted from Wolfman 2002, 59)

Folktales are tools for teaching cultural exploration and making personal connections. They provide universal themes, narrative power, and deep sociocultural underpinnings. Reading folktales also fosters strong home-school connections, intergenerational literacy, and bilingual growth. By taking turns doing repeated readings of folktales in two languages, parents and children together can develop fluency, familiarity, and pride in reading in both the home language and in English. Folktales can also be conveyed through dance and performed with Reader's Theater scripts. Folktales from around the world are readily available, both online and in beautiful hard copy renditions. (See Appendix C for suggestions.)

Making Personal Connections to Social Studies Text

State and national standards emphasize making personal, text-to-self connections to promote deep comprehension of complex texts. *Of Thee I Sing: A Letter to My Daughters* is a book that provides opportunities for students to make personal text-to-self connections in a rich social studies context (Obama 2010). This book explores many quintessentially American traits and ideals that have shaped our history, such as creativity, persistence, bravery, kindness, and strength. A powerful repeating refrain in the book is: "Have I told you that you are...creative, smart, brave, strong, kind, persistent, inspiring?" (Obama 2010).

To help students make personal connections to the text, teachers can follow these steps:

Personal Connections

1. Show the list of character traits from *Of Thee I Sing*:

creative	smart	respectful
strong	kind	persistent
inspiring	brave	a healer
an explorer	a singer	
a family member	an American	

2. Have each student choose one quality or trait listed above that best describes him or her.

3. Have each student dictate or write expansively and descriptively about the trait that describes him or her best by:

   - guiding students to focus their writing on one specific incident in their lives in which they clearly demonstrated the trait, and

   - guiding students to include detailed examples of their own specific behavior in a particular setting and situation.

4. Remind students that their goal is to include as many well-developed, specific details and examples as possible in order to convince readers that they demonstrate the trait.

5. Have students reread what they wrote and edit or revise as needed.

6. Have students read their personal writing to partners, a small group, or the whole class.

Analyzing Rhetorical Devices in Speeches

Teachers can use rhythm and repetition to help students meet another important new goal: analyzing rhetorical devices in speeches. To accomplish this, first introduce some major rhetorical devices in essays and speeches, which often use parallel construction in which key words are repeated using the same part of speech. Frequently repeated rhythmic phrases are especially effective rhetorical devices found in many famous speeches.

Parallelism means using the same part of speech and the same type of rhythmic phrasing in a series of sometimes repeating grammatical constructions.

Rhythmic repetition is used by presidents and other public speakers because the repeated rhythms and phrases make it easier for an audience to listen and remember the speech. An example of this rhetorical device is Dr. Martin Luther King, Jr.'s famous repeated refrain, "I have a dream, I have a dream that—." The rhythmic cadence of the repetition enables audiences to follow King's main ideas and remember his inspiring words decades later.

To access King's "I Have a Dream" speech and 100 other top speeches, visit www.americanrhetoric.com/speeches/mlkihaveadream.htm

To begin a lesson on rhetorical devices in speeches, point out the parallelism and repetition of rhythmic refrains in portions of King's speech as shown in Figure 4.3. Then, in a gradual release of responsibility, have students locate these rhetorical devices with a partner and, finally, locate them on their own.

Figure 4.3 Portion of "I Have A Dream" Speech by Martin Luther King, Jr. (August 28, 1963)

Let freedom ring from the mighty mountains of New York.
Let freedom ring from the heightening Alleghenies of Pennsylvania.
Let freedom ring from the snow-capped Rockies of Colorado.
Let freedom ring from the curvaceous slopes of California.
But not only that:
Let freedom ring from Stone Mountain of Georgia.
Let freedom ring from Lookout Mountain of Tennessee.
Let freedom ring from every hill and molehill of Mississippi.
From every mountainside, let freedom ring.
I have a dream that one day on the red hills of Georgia, the sons of former slaves and the sons of former slave owners will be able to sit down together at the table of brotherhood.
I have a dream that one day even the state of Mississippi, a state sweltering with the heat of injustice, sweltering with the heat of oppression, will be transformed into an oasis of freedom and justice.
I have a dream that my four little children will one day live in a nation where they will not be judged by the color of their skin but by the content of their character.

Some useful steps for teaching analysis of rhetorical devices in speeches are:

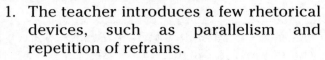

Analyzing Rhetorical Devices

1. The teacher introduces a few rhetorical devices, such as parallelism and repetition of refrains.

2. The teacher presents portions of three famous speeches.

3. Students find examples of the rhetorical devices in the three speeches and determine which speech they think is most effective from a rhetorical perspective.

4. Students explain their reasons, making specific references from the texts of the speeches as evidence to support their positions.

(Adapted from ReadWriteThink 2015)

Using Digital Technology and Multimodal Teaching

College and Career Readiness standards aim to help students develop the ability to create arguments and support their arguments with credible evidence. Another goal of the standards is to infuse digital technology into the 21st century social studies curriculum. Julie Wise and Alexandra Panos (2014) do an excellent job of demonstrating how to use digital technology effectively in conjunction with books, artwork, magazines, and articles to create multimodal history projects.

Creating Multimodal Arguments

To begin, Wise and Panos (2014) suggest that teachers create a multimodal history text set around a specific point of view on a topic. The text set can include a textbook, artwork, short passages with views that differ from those in the textbook, and digitized primary sources. A wide range of technology tools and software programs are available for multimodal projects, including:

- PowerPoint Slideshow
- Movie Maker
- Photo Story
- iMovie
- VoiceThread.com
- Animoto.com

A *multimodal argument* is the presentation of a thesis with a clear point of view—utilizing various modes, such as expository writing, poetry, song, rap, movement, dance, images, and video. As with traditionally written expository arguments, multimodal arguments are presented and supported by logical, clearly presented details and evidence. The main difference is that multimodal arguments include digital evidence. To help students begin this type of technology project, have them watch an example of a multimodal argument presented in the form of a documentary film. Here's one way to guide students through the first viewing:

1. Identify the author's perspective.

2. Identify the author's claims.

3. Identify the evidence.

4. Identify the closing argument.

Next, have students watch the film again, this time with different purposes. During the second viewing, direct students to think critically about how different modes, such as sounds, images, movement, and words work together. Have students consider the following questions about the various modes of presentation. These types of questions promote the ability to consider the role of multiple modes of collecting and presenting social studies ideas, a skill emphasized in state and national standards.

- Which modes of presentation does the author use?

- How does each mode enhance the mood, theme, and claims of the main argument?

- Were any of the modes distracting to the argument? If so, which ones? Why?

- What techniques do you want to try in your own multimodal argument project? (Adapted from Wise and Panos 2014)

To teach students how to make a coherent argument with digital resources, modeling by the teacher is crucial. To begin, use a storyboard or whiteboard to compose the argument. Provide structure to the process by guiding students through the following steps:

1. State a claim clearly. Know the main idea and communicate it well.

2. Model ways to support the claim with specific evidence.

   - Include evidence from the text(s), giving credit where credit is due.

   - Include evidence from the primary digital sources, including texts, images, and music. Give credit to the filmmaker, videographer, singer, actor, or artist during the presentation.

3. Provide a concluding statement that briefly summarizes the main ideas(s) or asks an interesting question of the audience.

4. Demonstrate ways to include a narrative to explain the main points of the argument; for example, tell about a few interesting examples as a way to expand and explain the main points.

After the teacher models and students create their own digital, multimodal argument projects, have them present their projects to the class, the school, or an audience of friends and family. Remind students that each multimodal presentation of historical arguments must include a clear claim, credible evidence, a clear conclusion, and a critical self-analysis of their own experience learning from the multimodal process.

Multimodal history projects provide a timely and important focus on critical thinking and writing activities. These projects can promote deeper understanding of historical argumentation and presentation skills, a key focus of Common Core State Standards. While classmates present their digital/multimodal history projects, students in the audience can write responses to the presentations. This ensures active attention and involvement and enhances learning. It's helpful to provide students with questions to guide their listening and viewing, such as:

- What is the stance or viewpoint of each argument? How do you know? What evidence do you notice?

- Which modes of presentation evoked feelings of anger and annoyance or sympathy and agreement?

- How did the multimodal presentation affect your view of this historical event?

- Was the digital material a helpful aid, or was it a distraction? Why? If it was a distraction or seemed like extraneous "window dressing," how could the digital material be used more effectively in future presentations? (Adapted from Wise and Panos 2014)

Integrating Peer Observation Feedback

Since state and national standards focus on research and presentation skills, many social studies units today require students to conduct research about a topic and then present what they learned to the class. How can teachers ensure that students in the audience are attentive and learn from their classmates' oral presentations? One of the best ways to encourage audience participation and attention is to expect listeners to give both oral and written feedback to their peers. By using a specific feedback form, such as the one in Figure 4.4, students in the audience listen more attentively, learn more from each other, and become adept at presenting information orally, analyzing the style and content of presentations, and giving and receiving constructive feedback. These lessons are invaluable not only for social studies units and learning across the curriculum, but for success throughout life.

Using Technology to Analyze Multiple Perspectives

Students need guidance in learning how to analyze multiple perspectives in digital materials. Teachers can begin by guiding students to identify points of agreement and disagreement across multiple texts, images, and video clips. For example, the teacher can find two digital materials that differ in perspective regarding American Indians and land. One digital text might acknowledge the controversy over land ownership and the removal of American Indians from their land in the 1830s. In contrast, another might address the topic superficially or omit any mention of this ongoing controversy.

After students have analyzed different perspectives about the same issue using different sources, have them identify their own stance in response to an argument prompt. To help them, ask questions such as the ones that follow. These types of questions promote critical-thinking skills and help students consider multiple perspectives about historical arguments, including their own.

Questions for analyzing different perspectives are often geared for secondary students. However, younger students should also be introduced to this analytical thinking approach using topics about which the students are very familiar. Teachers should select and modify questions to fit the needs and abilities of their students.

- Do you think the removal of American Indians during the 1830s was necessary? Why?

- Do you think Abraham Lincoln did enough to end slavery? Why?

- Do you think the 1960s civil rights movement ended discrimination against African Americans in the United States? Why? What more remains to be done to end prejudice and discrimination? How do you know?

- Do you think the United States should have entered World War II earlier than it did? Why?

- Do you think the internment of Japanese-Americans in prison camps during World War II was necessary? Do you think it was consistent with American ideals? Why?

- Do you think American involvement in the Vietnam War was a good decision? Why?

- Do you think American involvement in the wars in Iraq and Afghanistan was a good decision? Why?

Using Team-Based Learning (TBL)

Research shows that learning social studies in teams is both effective and fun (Klingner et al. 2014; Wanzek et al. 2014). Jeanne Wanzek, Sharon Vaughn, Shawn Kent, and their colleagues advocate a highly effective team approach, called Team-Based Learning (TBL) (Wanzek et al. 2014). This strategy delineates each student's role and responsibilities clearly in order to maximize participation and results. For example, if a class is studying the Great Depression, the teacher might divide the class into small groups of four students in each group. If each group has the task to research, summarize, and present its findings to the whole class, the class would likely benefit from using a TBL framework. This approach clarifies each participant's job and ensures active participation of each group member. The details of roles and responsibilities of each group participant in TBL are:

- Lead Facilitator: Elicits meaningful participation from each team member; keeps team on task.

- Text Source Facilitator: Guides the team through the process of reading relevant text, analyzing it, and locating the best evidence to support the team's answers to unit questions.

- Synthesizer: Listens to competing ideas; helps team resolve differences; synthesizes the ideas presented.

- Product Manager: Organizes team materials; is responsible for final products (answer sheets and written responses); reports team decisions to the class.

Conclusion

Social Studies has the power to transform and affect each student profoundly—intellectually, socially, and emotionally. The reason is that social issues pop up everywhere—not only in textbooks and biographies, but also in our daily lives at home, at school, and at work. Check the news online, in print, or on other media, and each day you learn about new challenges facing our country and our world.

Teaching social studies in the 21st century can be fulfilling and exciting. By integrating rhythm, singing, drawing, rap, dance, and drama into the curriculum, teachers can add a new dimension that reinforces and enriches lessons and enables all types of students to succeed in social studies and care about social issues.

Reflect and Discuss

1. What activities, strategies, and materials from the chapter are you most excited to use with your students?

2. How can these strategies help students make a personal connection with history?

3. Think of an upcoming social studies unit. Select two strategies or activities that you'd like to include. What planning and preparation do you need to do in order to be successful?

Chapter 5

Reading, Writing, and Rhythm in Math

Questions to Activate Thinking

1. What excites you most about teaching math?

2. How do you currently make math fun and engaging for students?

3. What challenges you most about math instruction?

4. In what ways can you use movement to help build students' conceptual understanding?

Teaching Math in the 21st Century

Today's math teachers face great challenges. Teaching math in the 21st century entails teaching new math skills, teaching traditional math skills in new ways, and simultaneously weaving in literacy lessons. Math teachers today are expected to teach students digital skills, speaking and listening skills, critical thinking, analytical and problem-solving skills, and the ability to reflect on their own mathematical development. Moreover, math teachers need to show students that mathematical knowledge is essential to their future success at home, at work, and in social situations.

This chapter presents exciting ways to engage K–12 students in mathematics through interesting materials, challenging projects, and enticing hands-on activities that make math come alive. The activities and resources align with state and national standards in both literacy and mathematics. The chapter emphasizes general academic literacy and domain-specific mathematics literacy, with a focus on mathematical word meanings, concepts, and skills.

Exploring Math Attitudes

Student Attitudes

Poetry has the power to move us deeply and delve into our own emotions and attitudes, including our emotions and attitudes toward math. We know that some students have negative feelings about math stemming from early frustrations with math in school. Carl Sandburg's poem "Arithmetic" in Figure 5.1 captures such feelings of math frustration in a light-hearted way. This poem is funny while it demonstrates authentic feelings and math experiences that resonate with students of all ages.

> **Figure 5.1 Excerpt from "Arithmetic" by Carl Sandburg**
>
> Arithmetic is where numbers fly like pigeons out of your head....
>
> ...Arithmetic is where you have to multiply—and you carry the multiplication table in your head and hope you won't lose it.
>
> ...If you ask your mother for one fried egg for breakfast and she gives you two fried eggs and you eat both of them, who is better at arithmetic, you or your mother?

(Adapted from Hendrick and Hendrick 1996)

After reading Sandburg's poem, students can write about their own personal math experiences, both positive and negative, during in-class free-writes, essays, sentence completion activities, and poetry activities. Then, students can share what they wrote and discuss their reactions with a partner or small group. Here's an activity about students' math memories that helps them develop skills in reading, writing, listening, and speaking while they explore the origins of their feelings and early experiences with math.

Math Attitudes

1. Have students begin by responding to the following prompts:

My Math Memories
- My earliest memory of math is_____.
- One of my favorite memories of math happened when _____.
- One of my worst math memories is _____.
- One of the most exciting math activities is _____.

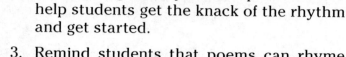

Math Attitudes *(cont.)*

2. Tell students to use their responses to fill in the blanks in the math poem frame below using 4/4 rhythm. Clap the beat to help students get the knack of the rhythm and get started.

3. Remind students that poems can rhyme but do not necessarily have to contain rhymes.

4. To help students get started, model one or two of the blanks that fit your own math experience. For example, "In kindergarten math was fun/We counted numbers and learned to write them/In first grade we learned to add and subtract/." (Note: This math poem prompt can be used in whole or in parts, depending on the grade.)

In kindergarten, math was _____.

We counted _____ and learned _____.

In first grade, math was _____.

We learned _____ and _____.

I liked/didn't like it and/but I _____.

Second grade was _____ and _____.

My teacher _____ and _____.

In third grade, we learned _____ and _____.

It was _____. I wanted to _____.

Fourth grade consisted of learning _____.

I did _____ then _____.

Math Attitudes *(cont.)*

The fifth-grade teacher taught us _____.

I did it _____, then learned to _____.

The sixth-grade teacher taught us _____.

I did it _____ and then I _____.

In seventh grade, we learned _____ also _____, _____, and _____.

Eighth-grade math was _____ and _____.

We finally learned _____.

In kindergarten, math was _____.

Now I find math is _____.

Teacher Attitudes

Research shows that students' perceptions of their teachers' attitudes toward math result in significant differences in students' math motivation and achievement (Levpuscek and Zupancic 2009). In fact, according to Levpuscek and Zupancic, a student's attitude toward math depends largely on the teacher's attitude. When a teacher conveys enthusiasm for math, students internalize the teacher's enthusiasm and do better (Jackson and Leffingwell 1999). Furthermore, if a teacher initially has self-doubt about teaching math but takes steps to prepare for the challenge, there are two positive outcomes: (1) improvement in the teacher's attitude, and (2) improvement in the teacher's ability to teach math effectively (Teague and Austin-Martin 1981). Clearly, the teacher's attitude matters.

The excerpt in Figure 5.2 from the poem "Passion" by Karen Morrow Durica (2007) underscores the teacher's influence. This poem can be used to spur discussions among teachers about the challenges and rewards of teaching math.

Figure 5.2 Excerpt from "Passion" (Durica 2007)

Who'd have thought that kids like us
Would get so into math?
We never liked those formulae
Or parabolic paths.
But the teacher assigned to algebra
Had fire in her eyes;
When she talked about equations,
We could see the fervor rise.

...Her excitement was contagious;
We were captured by her zest.
And in spite of hesitation,
We began to do our best.

We know that motivating students and getting them engaged in learning is instrumental to academic success in all content areas (Fink 2006; Fink and Samuels 2008; Guthrie, Klauda, and Ho 2013). To teach math (or any subject) effectively, the teacher needs to be good at motivating students. Using the self-reflection checklist in Figure 5.3 can help teachers to develop self-awareness as math motivators and make changes if necessary. This checklist can spur teachers to analyze their own part in the process of math motivation. After independently reflecting on the checklist, pairs or small groups of teachers can share their responses, using the checklist as a springboard for discussion. The goal of this activity is to develop self-awareness and realistic, positive attitudes that teachers can use to motivate all of their students, including reluctant math students as well as math stars.

Figure 5.3 Self-Reflection Checklist: How Good a Math Motivator Am I?

Yes	No	
		1. I believe my students are competent and can become more competent in mathematics with proper assistance.
		2. I attend to student interests and provide some level of choice in math class.
		3. I help students do things, learn how to do things, and talk about how to do things.
		4. I avoid labeling students whenever possible.
		5. I make good use of student experts in my class by getting students to teach each other and share their expertise.
		6. I use heterogeneous groups and interest groups to build interdependence, highlight student strengths, and use their different strengths.
		7. I communicate high math expectations to *all* of my students.
		8. I name the math skill or concept that students learn and master and focus on their mathematical abilities and achievements. I celebrate student expertise.
		9. I focus on future math success, not past failure.
		10. I foster math connections to students' current life concerns.
		11. I encourage fun and humor in math class and include the reading of humorous math texts.
		12. I use artifacts, concrete objects, and engaging hands-on activities in teaching math and ask students to create artifacts, concrete objects, songs, dramas, and so forth to help make math knowledge visible, reasoning accountable, and math activities engaging.
		13. I am passionate about the importance of teaching math, and I model and communicate my passion to my students.

(Adapted from Marsh and O'Neill 1984)

To maximize the benefits of the Self-Reflection Checklist, it's helpful to consider Carol Dweck's (2008) groundbreaking research on the role of mindset. Dweck divides people into two categories. One category consists of people who believe that intelligence, including mathematical intelligence, is static and inborn. This means that you are born either "good in math" or "not good in math," so your math ability is immutable, no matter what you do. One implication of this mindset is: Why try hard if no matter what I do, I just won't be good at math? In contrast, Dweck's second category consists of people who have what she calls a "growth mindset." These people believe that intelligence, including mathematical intelligence, can be improved. Dweck has shown that people with a growth mindset have a better trajectory for life success and do better academically in all subjects, including mathematics (Dweck 2008). Discussing Dweck's findings and her two categories can help frame discussions about the Self-Reflection Checklist. These discussions can help teachers explore ways to change their own mindset if they think it's appropriate.

Another way to follow up on the Self-Reflection Checklist is to discuss challenges and issues that the checklist raises. For example, if teachers label students in negative ways that result in lowered expectations, discuss what happens when students have teachers who do not lower expectations. My research on successful adults with severe dyslexia showed that they succeeded at high levels because a memorable teacher believed in them and did not lower expectations despite their labels (Fink 2006; Fink and Samuels 2008). Instead, they gave them extra help when needed.

Another way to follow up on the Self-Reflection Checklist is to discuss the close relationship between math attitudes and math teaching skills. Research suggests that teachers can improve their attitudes toward math and build strong math teaching skills simultaneously. As math attitudes improve, so too does math teaching performance (Teague and Austin-Martin 1981).

Moreover, teachers can take several steps to develop strong math teaching skills.

1. **Emphasize the connections of mathematics to everyday problems and tasks**. Teachers who do this succeed in making math meaningful and motivating for students (Cornell 1999).

2. **Include hands-on activities and student-directed lessons.** This also makes math meaningful and motivating (Cornell 1999).

3. **Let students see you in the process of figuring out a math problem.** Students benefit from seeing teachers genuinely engaged and struggling with math problems (Burks et al. 2009).

4. **Show students that you do not always have the "right answer" immediately.** This gives students an opportunity to witness your genuine problem-solving and critical reasoning in action in real-time (Burks et al. 2009).

Using Poetry to Teach Math Persistence

Success in any subject is linked to grit, or the ability to persevere despite frustrations (Tough 2012). Paul Tough (2012) and others have written about this crucial quality. Notable artists, statesmen, scientists, and inventors repeatedly proclaim that it was mainly their grit, hard work, and perseverance that enabled them to succeed. For example, Thomas Edison, the inventor of the light bulb and movie camera, famously said that success is 99 percent perspiration and only 1 percent inspiration. By this, Edison meant that his inventions were due to his grit, hard work, and refusal to give up when he ran into obstacles. Edison persevered despite the frustrations; inventing did not come easily to Edison but required persistence and hard work. Nothing captures the essence of Edison's message better than the poem "Try, Try Again" by T. H. Palmer (1847), shown in

Figure 5.4. Palmer's words encourage students to stick with it, try again, and persevere when learning math (or any subject) is difficult.

Figure 5.4 Excerpt from "Try, Try Again"

'Tis a lesson you should heed,
Try, try again;
If at first you do not succeed,
Try, try again;
Then your courage should appear,
For, if you will persevere,
You will conquer, never fear;
Try, try again.

After reading this short poem, students can do free-writes or short personal essays. Have them describe and analyze a personal math experience in which they persisted (or did not persist) when they faced difficulty learning a mathematical concept. For example, students may have had trouble mastering the multiplication tables. After they write about a specific math challenge, have students include strategies that helped them, and the extent to which they succeeded in mastering the math concept. Figure 5.5 provides a sample template to guide students as they analyze their own math experiences. After using the template as a guide for writing, students can share their writing with partners, discuss the consequences of persisting (or giving up), and consider the question, "What were the positive and negative outcomes?" These kinds of thought-provoking activities help students develop literacy skills while promoting self-awareness and deep understanding of their own approaches to math challenges. This self-awareness can lead to personal insight and changes that result in more positive attitudes and strategies that can last a lifetime.

Figure 5.5 Sample Template for Math Writing

In _____ grade, I had a math challenge in learning _____.
So I asked _____ to explain. However, unfortunately, _____.
Then I tried _____. This worked/didn't work for me. So I
learned/never learned to _____ well. This year I want to
learn _____ in math class. I plan to _____ to help me achieve
this math goal.

Literary fantasy is an effective genre for fostering positive attitudes and a zest for math. A great example is *The Number Devil: A Mathematical Adventure* (Enzensberger 2010). The protagonist of this fantasy is a boy named Robert, who hates math. Each night, Robert dreams about The Number Devil, who visits and cleverly lures him into solving intriguing math puzzles and problems. *The Number Devil* is funny and entertaining, and many students will relate easily to math-phobic Robert.

Teaching Math with Rhythm, Rhyme, Gesture, and Movement

Rhythm and Rhyme

Research suggests that rhythm and rhyme are powerful tools for creating deep memories (Silverman 2010). It follows that teachers can strengthen their math lessons by integrating rhythm and rhyme. It's easier to learn math facts and concepts through rhyming, and there are numerous catchy number rhymes for teaching counting and sequencing skills. One such rhyme, "One, Two, Buckle My Shoe," is a favorite of mine that I still remember my mother reciting to my sister. Teachers can use it to help young children meet goals for counting. And number concepts become especially memorable when teachers integrate creative movement and gestures to go along with each number set. For example, the teacher can model for students and perform the motions and gestures while reciting the lines of the poem "One, Two, Buckle My Shoe." The italics show how to use gesture and physical motions with "One, Two, Buckle My Shoe." The more the teacher hams up these activities with voice exaggeration and large body motions, the more students will enjoy them and learn from performing the poems and accompanying motions.

One, Two, Buckle My Shoe

One, two (*Hold up one finger, then two fingers*)
Buckle my shoe. (*Bend down low and pretend to buckle your shoe*)
Three, four (*Hold up three fingers, then four fingers*)
Knock on the door. (*Pretend to knock on a door*)
Five, six (*Hold up five fingers, then six fingers*)
Pick up sticks. (*Jump and then bend down low to pretend to pick up sticks*)
Seven, eight (*Hold up seven fingers, then eight fingers.*)
Do not be late. (*Point forefinger and shake it in a scolding motion*)
Nine, ten (*Hold up nine fingers, then 10 fingers*)
Let's count again! (*Make a two thumbs up motion, holding hands high*)

The italics on the next page show how to use body movement with the number rhyme "Inch, Inch, Inchin' Along" (adapted from Rakoncay 1987). In this engaging activity, students lie on the floor with their arms and legs stretched out in front and back of them. Since teacher modeling makes it easy for students to follow and learn, the teacher can help by demonstrating the positions and movements.

Inch, Inch, Inchin' Along

Look at me
1 2 3
I move as slowly as can be. (*Move slowly forward along the floor like an inchworm*)

Then I move some more
1 2 3 4
Crawlin' slowly 'cross the floor.

Chorus

Oh, it's a cinch (*Move on the floor in different directions*)
To be an inchworm,
Inch inch inchin' along.

Here I go, movin' slow. (*Move slowly forward on the floor*)
I move my front half first, you know. (*Lead movement with front half of body.*)
And when I get to where I want to be,
Then my back half catches up with me. (*Lower half of body moves forward to "catch up" with front half*)

Come with me (*Stand on two legs and reach arms high above head*)
1 2 3
Now we're inching up a tree. (*Reach on tiptoe with arms overhead, as if climbing a tree*)

And we'll look around (*Remain on tiptoe, move head from left to right as far as possible*)
Above the ground,
And then we'll inch our lazy way back down. (*Bend head, upper body, and knees so whole body is down on the floor in inchworm position*)

Chorus

1 2 3 4 5 6 (*Turn over on back, kick legs up in the air, alternating left foot and right foot*)
That's the way I get my kicks.
Inch by inch, don't you know (*Move slowly forward on belly along the floor*)
Inch by inch is the way to go.

1 2 3 4 5 6 7 (*Turn over on back, kick legs up in the air, alternating left foot and right foot*)
That's the way to get to heaven. (*Point to the sky*)
8 9 10 11 12 (*Kick legs up in the air, alternating left foot and right foot*)
Now we're looking for Santa's elves. (*Cup right hand over eyes as if looking for Santa's elves*)

13 14 15 16 (*Stand up and clap hands for each number*)
Now we're looking for some queens. (*Cup right hand over eyes as if looking for queens*)
17 18 19 20 (*Remain standing and clap hands while reciting each number*)
Sorry but there aren't any. (*Shake head "No" from left to right while raising palms of hands up and open to show "Empty"*)

Chorus (x2)

Creating Math Raps and Songs

A wonderful way to teach and reinforce math facts and procedures is with teacher-created raps and songs. In addition, student-created raps are a great way to help students consolidate what they've learned. Student- and teacher-made raps and songs can be used to review for weekly quizzes, midterms, or other tests and assessments. They're an excellent strategy for reviewing material to help students meet state and national goals and standards.

To create a math rap or song, follow these steps:

Creating Math Raps and Songs

1. Pick a well-known tune familiar to most students, such as "Yankee Doodle."

2. Record the key math facts or steps in a mathematical procedure that students need to learn. (Examples: 3 + 3 = 6 and other addition facts; 9 – 2 = 7 and other subtraction facts; multiplication tables, such as the 7 times table; and so forth.) (For further explanation about creating teacher-made raps, poems, or songs, see The Rap Protocol in Chapter 1.)

3. Write the relevant math facts in rhythm or rhyme, using the selected tune.

4. Teach students the words to the song and give them sufficient time in class to practice singing.

5. A fun follow-up activity is for students to perform the song for another class, the whole school, or an assembly to which family and friends are invited.

The 7 Times Song

by Rosalie Fink
(Sung to the tune of "Yankee Doodle")

7 x 1 is 7
7 x 2 is 14
7 x 3 is 21
I know my 7 times tables!
7, 14, 21,
28, 35,
42, 49,
56, yes, I know it!
7 x 4 is 28
7 x 5 is 35
7 x 6 is 42
I know my 7 times tables!
7, 14, 21,
28, 35,
42, 49,
56, yes, I know it!
7 x 7 is 49
7 x 8 is 56
7 x 9 is 63
7 x 10 equals 70
7, 14, 21,
28, 35,
42, 49,
56, yes I know it!

Using Gesture and Movement

An engaging way to develop number sense in young children is by having them sing, dance, and perform numbers. This can be done easily by using a variety of counting songs, such as "Ten Little Chickadees" (adapted from the tune "Ten Little Indians"). Each student represents one individual person, place, or thing, whether it is a chickadee, butterfly, lollipop, balloon, doll, or truck.

When conducting math dances, consider using scarves. A scarf is a terrific way to liberate students to move freely. I've found in my own classes that when students dance with scarves, it helps them move their bodies more fully, enabling them to extend their arms farther overhead or reach farther from side-to-side. In addition to promoting larger, freer body movements, a scarf can also be used effectively to denote costume and character—or even scenery.

Here are directions for conducting a math dance to the song "Ten Little Chickadees."

Conducting a Math Dance

1. Encourage students to dress up in the colors of their favorite chickadees.

2. Assign each student a number. Attach the number to the student's clothing.

3. Encourage each student to improvise a movement for flying like a chickadee.

4. The whole class sings the Chickadee song, substituting the word "chickadees" (or balls, dolls, lollipops, etc.) for "Indians."

5. While the class sings the song, the teacher calls on students one-by-one. As each student is called, he or she dances as if flying up to the front of the class. Provide a scarf for each student in order to add to the range and variety of arm motions, artistic expression, and fun.

Creating Interdisciplinary Lessons

Interdisciplinary lessons have been shown to engage students more and result in equal or better academic outcomes than single discipline curricula (Biancarosa and Snow 2006; Drake and Burns 2004). A wonderful book for interdisciplinary math and literacy lessons is *Curious George Learns to Count from 1 to 100* by H.A. Rey. This enticing, colorful text addresses many critical early grade math goals, such as number sense, reading numbers, counting skills, grouping, and mapping numbers. In this hilarious story, Curious George explores numbers in the naturalistic setting of his hometown and discovers that numbers and opportunities for counting are everywhere. Subtraction experiences and math and art activities using leaves and other forms of nature are also sprinkled throughout this Curious George story.

Curious George Learns to Count from 1 to 100 is excellent for simultaneously developing students' general academic vocabulary and domain-specific math vocabulary. To maximize students' vocabulary growth and text comprehension, teachers should discuss unfamiliar word meanings in the context of a meaningful sentence from the text before reading the story (Biancarosa and Snow 2006; Drake and Burns 2004). Examples from this Curious George story are:

1. Today is our town's *one-hundredth anniversary*.

2. George is having fun playing and counting on this *centennial* day.

3. George could not *resist* the *temptation*.

4. He *scampered* up the 40 *rungs* of the tall ladder.

After discussing the vocabulary, the teacher can pose questions that encourage students to think about the numbers. For example:

1. What is the highest number on this page?

2. What is the lowest number on this page?

3. What number do you think will be on the next page? Why?

4. Why do you think numbers are important in these sentences?

5. How would the meaning of this story change without the numbers?

While reading the book with a small group, the teacher can support students by reading and counting with them. This form of side-by-side modeling is effective with all types of students and is especially helpful for struggling readers, students with learning disabilities, and English language learners.

While reading *Curious George Learns to Count from 1 to 100*, teachers can use the numbers shown on each page to discuss number concepts in depth. For example, show students the picture of 13 socks and ask: Is that correct? When you count them, do you get 13 socks? Why is one sock a different color, and why is it funny to see 13 socks instead of 12 or 14? This is a good segue to discussing the concept of pairs. The teacher can follow up by discussing things that are grouped in other numerical combinations. (For example, a trio consists of three singers. A quartet has four musicians.) In this way, literacy learning and math learning become seamlessly linked in a natural, interdisciplinary manner.

After students read the book or any other book related to counting, have them practice skills to enhance their learning by playing a variety of games that involve counting as well as graphing activities (adapted from Rey 2005). These games are fun and provide opportunities for reinforcement of the number concepts.

Counting Games

Guess My Number

1. Think of a number in the range the students are learning. (For example, between 1–10 for young children, between 1–100 for older students.)

2. Children take turns guessing the number.

3. Each time a child guesses a number, the teacher says, "Higher" or "Lower" until students guess the number. This activity is good for kindergarten and early first grade, but can be easily adapted for second and early third-grade students. Simply change the activity to counting by 3s, 4s, 5s, 6s, 7s, 8s, and so forth.

4. Eventually, students can also play this game with partners or in small groups.

5. The Guess My Number Game can be adapted for older students into a place value game. To do this, the teacher thinks of a number and writes it down in pencil in a secure place (so that students know the teacher hasn't changed the number during the game or forgotten it). Then, a student guesses a two-digit number. The teacher writes it down on the board and tells the student how many digits the student guessed right and in how many places the digits were correctly placed. For example, if the number is 56 but a student guesses 64, the teacher explains that the student had one digit

Guess My Number *(cont.)*

right (6), but that it was in the wrong place, emphasizing the importance of place value.

Number Search

1. The teacher supplies magazines, newspapers, and advertising circulars and tells students to look for numbers and cut them out. Then, students report the numbers they found.

2. To add physical movement to this activity, students can take a walk around the classroom, outside the school, or in the hallway to look for numbers, just as Curious George did. When students return to the classroom, they report what numbers they found.

Walking Count

1. Take a walk and have each student count the number of steps he or she takes from one place to another. Older students can count the number of steps they take by twos, threes, fours, fives, sixes, and so forth. Students can also count the number of trees, flowers, cats, or dogs they see. Older students can be challenged to count by other numbers, such as fives, tens, and so forth.

2. An alternative is to choose something specific for students to count while they walk—sidewalk squares, houses, and trees (just as Curious George did).

Count Around the House

1. Tell students to count at home.

2. Ask, "What can you count in your home that George counted in his?"

3. Ask, "Do you have fewer or more of these items than George did?"

Skip Counting

1. Group items by twos, fives, and tens whenever possible. For example, when teaching about money, the teacher can use toy money from Monopoly to give students practice counting bills in different denominations, such as $5, $10, $20, $100, and so forth.

2. Encourage students to deal cards by twos, fives, or tens when playing card games.

Graphing Activity

Curious George Learns to Count from 1 to 100 presents a great opportunity to teach the meaning of graphs and how to create graphic displays. After students count items, teachers can guide them to make a graph of various items in the book. For example, have students graph: 6 toy boats, 7 cars, 15 blue tiles, 9 stuffed animals, 8 trucks, 16 rubber ducks, 14 shoes, and 12 ties. Then, ask questions such as: Are there more stuffed animals than cars? How do you know? Are there fewer shoes than ties? How do you know?

Making Number Books

A great way to get young students excited about numbers is to have them create personal number books. This activity helps students meet early math goals of learning number sense, learning to count, and learning to read and write numbers. Creating number books also helps students develop confidence and pride in their math abilities and become more engaged in reading and math. Most students love showing their very own number books to friends and family.

Here's how to help them make their own number books:

Number Books

1. Bring in discarded magazines for students to explore, looking for pictures of things of interest to them.

2. Create a book using construction paper. The teacher can collect the necessary materials in advance: piles of multi-colored construction paper, staplers with staples, scissors, paste, and magic markers or crayons. The teacher may want to staple 5–8 pages of construction paper together in advance to form blank books. Tell students to use both sides of the construction paper to save paper. Then, have students write a number from 1–10 or 1–20 (or whatever range of numbers the class is studying) at the top of each page.

3. Encourage students to cut out pictures from the magazines that represent different numbers of items of interest. For example, if a student is interested in dolls, he or she can find and cut out pictures of as many dolls as possible. Encourage students to cut and paste any item that interests them, including trucks, cars, balls, boats, fire engines, police cars, rubber ducks, dogs, cats, dresses, shoes, and so forth.

4. In most cases, the first page of the number book will have the number 1. Direct the student to cut out one item and have the student paste one item on the paper to match the number on the top of the page—in this case one. Repeat for all the numbers in the book until every page is illustrated with the corresponding number of cut-out items.

5. Have students read their counting books to partners. For example, the child reads the number aloud, such as "1", and then says "1 doll" or "1 truck," depending on the particular cut-out object. Afterwards, the teacher can encourage students to take home their counting books and read them to family or friends.

6. Display all of the counting books in the classroom or in the school's hallway for all to see. This helps students develop pride and confidence in their math and literacy accomplishments.

Creating Comics

Two websites that have links with suggestions for creating comics are:

- ReadWriteThink.org Comic Creator (www.readwritethink.org/files/resources/interactives/comic/cartoon10.swf)
- Pixton (www.pixton.com/)

Many students today are interested in comic books and graphic novels; they seem to gravitate naturally to these visually appealing texts. Such "out of school" texts are powerful teaching tools that can easily be used to teach content subjects such as math facts and concepts (Hong Xu 2008). Using comics and graphic novels is a great way to motivate students and help them discover, learn, reinforce, and apply mathematical concepts while they learn literacy skills. Creating mathematical comic strips simultaneously helps students learn math, literacy, and oral performance skills. It's another great way to teach math and literacy together in a seamless fashion. Steps for creating a math comic strip are (Adapted from Altieri 2011):

1. Decide on the goal or specific information students should learn from the comic strip, such as:
   - learn a strategy for solving word problems,
   - learn how to explain a math process, or
   - teach or reinforce a math fact (Examples: $3 + 3 = 6$; $5 \times 5 = 25$).

2. Bring in several popular comic strips that students enjoy. Teachers can use old newspapers or magazines, or collect comic strips from the local library or a coffee shop's discarded comics.

3. Distribute the comic strips, giving students a chance to examine them closely.

4. Brainstorm a list of the common features of comic strips with the whole class, discussing each feature. Features usually include:
   - text bubbles
   - limited words
   - illustrations
   - frames
   - captions
   - dialogue (usually between two characters)

5. Tell students that they will create their own comic strips and that each comic strip should have a particular mathematical learning purpose. For example, each comic strip needs to teach or review a particular math concept, such as addition and subtraction facts.

6. In planning a math comic strip activity, give students choices between working in pairs or working by themselves, and encourage them to use technology to create their comic strips. If they lack Internet access, have students use index cards to create the individual frames of their comic strips. Then have them put the frames in order on a large sheet of paper.

7. Have students share their comic strips with partners, small groups, or the whole class. While they share, guide them to explain why they created the comics the way they did. Have the audience ask questions and give constructive feedback about the presenter's comic strip. Encourage student feedback by asking the following questions:

- What is the math message?

- How successful is this comic strip in conveying this math message?

- What made this comic strip successful? What were its strong points?

- How might this comic strip be revised to make the math message clearer?

Teaching Math with Children's Literature

A compelling way to draw students to math is through high quality children's literature. Teachers can do three things to help students get the most from reading math-related literature:

1. **Present important vocabulary words in context** and discuss the words before reading the book. This activates students' prior knowledge and helps them form the habit of using the context to enhance their understanding.

2. **Ask thought-provoking questions**, and have students respond in writing. They can also share their responses with a partner, a small group, or the whole class. This promotes critical thinking, close reading of text, and deep understanding.

3. **Provide frequent opportunities for students to explain and justify their responses** based on the text and/or their own experiences. This activity encourages close reading of the text.

An example of a wonderful way to apply math measurement skills is to read, measure, and cook with *Fairy Tale Feasts* (Yolen and Stemple 2009). This captivating book contains classic folktales and fairy tales as well as delicious recipes to go with each tale. Each recipe requires careful, precise measurement, so that students learn to apply their math skills in real-life situations.

Another excellent book that integrates literacy and math for students in kindergarten and first grade is *The Action of Subtraction* by Brian Cleary (2008). Cleary's terrific sense of humor shines throughout this engaging book, which matches clever rhyming verse with comical cartoon cats to teach the concept of subtraction. This book is excellent for teaching lessons on subtraction, which can be reinforced by playing Take It Away!

Take It Away!

1. The teacher introduces the following subtraction problem with decomposing numbers (regrouping) by discussing the previous lessons on subtraction as well as strategies for regrouping numbers.

2. The teacher introduces the new problem: John and Maria went outside and jumped rope during recess. John jumped 43 times with a jump rope. Maria jumped 8 times fewer than John. How many times did Maria jump?

3. The teacher asks students to consider the following:

   - What does *fewer* mean?

   - How might you solve this problem?

   - What strategies do you think you want to try? Why?

4. Students think about the meaning of the word *fewer* in the context of this number story involving subtraction. Then they think about a method they could use to solve the problem in this number story. Next, they work to solve the problem.

Take It Away! *(cont.)*

5. The teacher walks around the room noticing various ways that students are solving the problem. If students are struggling, ask questions such as, "Can you tell me what you're doing? What do you know so far about this problem? What does the word *fewer* mean? How would you write the problem?"

6. Students discuss and share their ideas with a partner.

7. Then the teacher tells students to write down their approach and show their work by solving the problem in writing. Next, the teacher directs students to check their work.

8. The teacher notices students' various approaches and addresses any incorrect solutions or misconceptions by discussing the errors or having another student with a correct response explain.

9. The teacher ends by sharing the correct answer. Effective approaches for regrouping in subtraction problems are repeated and emphasized as the lesson concludes.

(Adapted from Ortega 2010)

Scaffolding Close Reading through Questions

We know from research that higher-level questions (such as inferential and open-ended questions) are essential for scaffolding the ability to read complex texts with deep comprehension (De Temple and Snow 1998; Snow 2010). Therefore, teachers today are being encouraged to integrate three types of comprehension questions into their daily lessons. These types of questions help maximize students' growth in both literacy and math skills from reading math-related literature. For example:

- **factual questions** can be located in the text; they are "right there on the page" in most cases;

- **inferential questions** are not "right there;" however, clues and hints to inferential questions can often be found "on the page;" and

- **open-ended questions** require thinking beyond the text; these questions often have more than one correct answer.

Directed reading and questioning lessons that include all three levels of questions enable students to engage in close reading of complex texts that contain challenging math concepts. For example, a close reading lesson based on the marvelous book, *The Boy Who Loved Math: The Improbable Life of Paul Erdos* (Heligman 2013), could include the following questions:

Literal/Factual Questions
(Look Right There on the Page)

- Where did Paul Erdos live as a boy? (After students find the answer, have them locate Budapest, Hungary on a map or globe.)

- What are negative numbers?

- How did Paul learn about negative numbers?

- What is a prime number?

- What questions did Paul have about prime numbers?

- How many seconds have you been alive? How could you find out?

- Is the number of minutes you've been alive a prime number?

- Why did so many people all around the world love Paul?

- What inventions resulted from the math problems that Paul Erdos and his friends figured out how to solve?

Inferential Questions
(Use Clues to Guess)

- Why did Paul like numbers?

- What do you think Paul meant when he said that his mother would spend 100 percent of her time with him during the summer? How much is 100 percent?

- How do you think Paul was able to figure out how many seconds the visitor in the story had been alive?

- Why do you think Paul invented his own way to live?

- How did Paul estimate that he did math about 133 hours each week?

- How do you think Paul felt upon learning that his mother was going back to work soon? Why do you think he felt this way?

Open-Ended Questions
(Think Beyond the Text)

- Do you like numbers? Why?

- Do you think you would like to become a mathematician? Why?

- Do you think that negative numbers are cool, like Paul? Why?

- What do you think our world would be like if we did not have numbers?

- Paul Erdos and his friends worked on number theory, combinatorics, the probabilistic method, and set theory. What do you think these might be? How could you find out?

- What else would you like to know about Paul Erdos or other mathematicians?

The math concept of prime numbers is a key concept in *The Boy Who Loved Math*. After teaching the concept, help students review prime numbers by teaching them "The Prime Numbers Rap" by Kyleena Harper as shown below.

The Prime Numbers Rap

by Kyleena Harper

It's smart to know the difference between composites and primes.
That's the whole reason behind this rhyme.
Knowing the difference will help you out
When finding the factors of a number, no doubt.
A prime number can be divided
By itself and 1—
That's it, no other numbers,
Just itself and 1!

I know we just started, we've just begun,
But I have to tell you, before you run,

There's 25 primes between 100 and 1,
And knowin' them will help you in the long run.

We start with 2, 3, 5, and 7.
What comes next? You're right, 11!
13 and 17 come next—
Knowing these numbers will help you pass the test.
19, 23, then 29—
You're doing great, you're doing better than fine!

31, 37, and 41—
Look at you, are you having fun?
43, 47, 53—
We're doing great on this prime number spree!

59 is next, then 61—
Great news kids, we're almost done!
67, 71, we're gettin' close,
But be sure to stay sharp and on your toes.
73 is next, then 79—
Almost there, now we're startin' to shine,

Then 83 and 89—
Look at that, just in time,

Because 97 is your last.
Knowing your primes makes you top o' the class!

Research Mathematicians

The Boy Who Loved Math is likely to spark students' curiosity about mathematicians as people since it recounts Erdos' relationships with important people in his life: his mother, his nanny, and his many friends around the world. After reading the story, students can learn more by doing Internet research on the life of Paul Erdos or the lives of other mathematicians in the book. To guide students' searches, have them find:

- facts about the mathematician's life
- a major mathematical discovery
- the significance of the mathematical discovery
- surprising information they learned
- a question they would like to ask the mathematician
- other questions they have about math and this individual

The following list of mathematicians who interacted with Erdos or were influenced by his work provides a jumping off point as students begin their research projects on a mathematician of interest. Some outstanding mathematicians mentioned in the book are:

Penny E. Haxell	Imre Barany
Linda Lesniak	Alfred Tarski
Paul Turan	Solomon W. Golomb
Albert Einstein	Alfred Renyi
Vera T. Sos	Carl Pomerance
Fan Chung	Cecil C. Rousseau
Ravindran Kannan	Andras Sarkozy
Andrew Chi-chih Yao	Esther Szerkeres
Andras Hajnal	Igor Shparlinski
Laszlo Lovasz	

Teaching Tier 2 and Tier 3 Mathematics Vocabulary

An important way to promote success for all students is to provide explicit vocabulary instruction and lots of practice with general academic vocabulary words frequently used across content areas. These words are sometimes referred to as Tier 2 words. Teachers should include explicit instruction in Tier 2 general academic words, such as *explain, analyze, summarize, justify,* and so forth (Snow 2002). In addition, give explicit instruction in what are known as Tier 3 words. These words are domain-specific words used with precise meanings in the context of each content area. For example, Tier 3 math words include *add, subtract, multiply, divide, decimal, regroup, product, inch, foot, meter, centimeter, minute, hour, right angle, rectangle, perimeter,* and so forth.

Professor Catherine Snow of Harvard and her colleagues urge teachers to use every opportunity possible to teach the meanings of general academic vocabulary words (such as "analyze") as well as specialized math vocabulary (such as "multiply") (Lawrence et al. 2014). Snow advises that vocabulary instruction be intentional and planned, not sporadic and left to chance (Snow, Lawrence, and White 2009). Research shows that even when young children seem to develop adequate reading fluency in grades K–2, they often fall behind later if they lack sufficient academic vocabulary knowledge (Chall 1996). This usually becomes apparent in third or fourth grade, when the curriculum becomes more demanding and requires students to "read to learn" (Chall 1996).

Educators have discovered that in order for a person to understand a word deeply and be able to integrate a new word and use it in speaking or writing, numerous exposures to the word are necessary (Lawrence et al. 2014). This means that math teachers need to teach lessons devoted explicitly to math vocabulary instruction. It also means providing students with numerous opportunities and experiences with each new mathematical term.

Vocabulary in Children's Literature

Introducing general academic vocabulary and domain-specific math vocabulary from children's literature can be done through the Syllabication for Decoding Strategy (SDS) shown in the sentences that follow. This strategy can be used for students of all ages who need decoding instruction and practice but it is especially helpful for struggling readers, students with learning disabilities, and English language learners. (More details about the Syllabication for Decoding Strategy are explained in Chapter 2.) Here are a few examples of how to use SDS with *The Boy Who Loved Math*:

- Mama loved Paul to *infinity* (3). (in/fi/ni/ty—four beats or syllables) After discussing the mathematical meaning of *infinity*, ask, "How much do you think Paul's mama loved him? How can you tell from the pictures and the words? How does the author use the word *infinity* on page 3? What does the author mean there?"

- Paul knew he had to *tackle* a big problem (7). (tac/kle—two beats or syllables) After discussing the general meaning of *tackle,* ask, "How do you think tackling a math problem differs from tackling a football player?"

Math Vocabulary Notebooks

Math vocabulary notebooks are wonderful for providing the multiple exposures to words that lead to mastery of math vocabulary. With this strategy, each student makes a personal math vocabulary notebook. Words for the book can include words from the student's math text as well as other math words introduced in class. Here are steps for using this approach:

1. The teacher writes new math vocabulary words on the board while introducing the words to the class. (Some examples of mathematical terms include *proportion, parallel,* and *quadrilateral.*)

2. The students copy the words into their notebooks.

3. Students look up the definition of each word in the glossary of the math textbook or in a dictionary. Alternatively, the teacher provides a definition for each math word.

4. Students use each word in a correct, meaningful sentence. They write their sentences in their math vocabulary notebooks, underlining the math vocabulary word.

5. Students add to their notebooks any additional words they encounter in their math texts.

6. The teacher encourages students to refer to their notebooks as they read the text and study for math tests.

To provide the multiple exposures and opportunities to work with new math vocabulary that students need (Snow 2002), teachers can choose from the following activities that build math vocabulary on a daily basis (Adapted from Dipple 2015):

Math Vocabulary Activities

- Encourage group work so that students hear others' ideas and hear math vocabulary spoken often.

- Share what you hear. For example, the teacher can circulate among groups of students while they work and say, "In this group, I heard _____."

- Build a Math Word Wall in the classroom.

- Have a Math Word of the Day.

- Make Math Word Webs. Give students a math word and have them brainstorm with a partner or small group as many words as they can that go with that word.

- Sort and label: Identify important math words for a unit, and have partners or small groups sort the words into categories based on their specific mathematical meanings. Then, have students decide on a title or label and present and justify their groupings to the class.

- Everyday Math Vocabulary: Teach specific lessons for math vocabulary words that have different meanings in everyday language and math. For example: foot, angle, factor, mean, and so forth.

Math Bingo

Many literacy goals focus on helping students learn Tier 2 general academic vocabulary as well as Tier 3 math words. Tier 3 entails learning mathematical terms and concepts and understanding them deeply, not just superficially. Playing Math Bingo is an engaging way to help students gain an understanding of math vocabulary and experience the multiple exposures to new words necessary for meaningful comprehension. Here are steps for setting up Math Bingo after teaching the new vocabulary beforehand (Adapted from Baines and Kunkel 2000):

Math Bingo

1. The teacher selects 25 mathematical terms that students need to know and writes each term on a slip of paper. The slips are placed in a box or bowl.

2. The teacher writes the words on the board.

3. Each student draws a bingo sheet with five columns and five rows.

4. Students then fill in each square on their sheets with one of the terms from the board in random order. The teacher reminds students not to copy the words in exact order from the board.

5. The teacher selects the first word and reads the definition, or reads a sentence that uses the word in a meaningful context.

6. Students mark that word on their bingo sheets.

7. Continue the steps above until a student completes a whole column of five words and calls out, "Bingo!"

8. The student who calls "Bingo!" must read each word from the bingo column, give a correct definition, and use it correctly in a sentence. If the student succeeds, then that student wins the game.

Assessing Math Comprehension through Journal Writing

We know that it's important for students to engage in self-reflection about their own learning (Dewey 1997; Costa and Kallick 2008). Math journal writing is one of the best ways for students to accomplish this goal, because writing a math journal requires that students pause and think deeply about a mathematical concept. Math journal writing is also an excellent way for students and teachers to assess a student's learning process and how well a student understands a particular math concept. This journaling technique simultaneously advances a student's mathematical skills and writing ability.

According to Haltiwanger and Simpson (2013), giving students in the middle and high school grades regular opportunities to write in math class promotes their critical thinking and awareness of math connections; it also results in clearer communication skills, especially when students share their journals with peers. Here's one way to incorporate journal writing into regular math lessons:

Math Journals

1. The teacher gives a writing prompt or question based on a recent math lesson, such as, "How would you tell somebody to solve the following problem:

   $3x + 4x = 35?$"

2. Students write responses in their math journals for about 5–8 minutes.

3. Students exchange journals with partners and read each other's journal entries.

4. Students write comments and/or give verbal feedback to each other. For example, students can be directed to say, "One thing that I learned from your journal is _____." They can also say, "One thing that I liked about your journal is _____."

5. Students then ask one question about a specific aspect or part of the journal. For example, students might say, "I'm not sure what you mean by _____. Tell me more about _____." The teacher should explain to students that an aspect that raises a question is usually a section of the journal that needs further explanation and development to make its meaning clear. (For more details, see Chapter 2 for a protocol on how to give and receive constructive peer feedback on writing.)

6. Students revise their journals based on their partners' questions and suggestions.

7. Students then hand in their journals to the teacher, who uses the journal entries to assess how well each student understands the math material, noting the subtopics that need further explanation.

Optional: The teacher grades the journal response based on predetermined criteria shared with the class. Criteria could include:

- demonstration of mastery of the math concept

- responsiveness to peer feedback

- improvement in clarity of written explanations

Using a Problem-Solving Process Approach

State and national standards stress not only procedural math skills, such as how to add, subtract, multiply, and divide, but also conceptual understanding and problem solving. To encourage the development of conceptual understanding and problem-solving skills, teachers need to establish a learning environment conducive to problem solving—one that is motivating, relaxed, and open to creative mathematical thinking and experimentation. There are several key things to consider (Adapted from Eckert and Leimbach 1993):

- Create a relaxed, comfortable learning environment for all types of students by encouraging active involvement of English language learners, students with learning disabilities, "typically developing" students, and advanced learners.

- Encourage a creative approach to learning mathematics, rather than a totally prescriptive, lock-step routine approach. This means encouraging all types of questions from all types of students and exploring a variety of ways to approach the math curriculum. Emphasize creative thinking and conceptual understanding, not just memorization of formulae.

- Tell students that it is okay for them to be puzzled by a mathematical word problem, and explain that professional mathematicians are puzzled by math problems, too.

- Allow sufficient time for students to work on math word problems. This requires differentiation for students who work quickly and those who work at a slower pace.

- Encourage students to experiment with different strategies in order to find ones that work for them.

- Provide lots of opportunities for students to work together to share ideas on problem solving. Give frequent, short "partner periods" during whole-class lessons, when students discuss their guesses or solutions to problems with their partners. This can take one or two minutes. It can also involve longer sessions during which small groups (3–6 students) work cooperatively on a solution. If, for example, problems require measurement, groups of students can work together measuring and recording their measurements systematically. Based on the needs and abilities of the class, the teacher needs to use judgment about the format and length of time allotted.

- Encourage students to talk about the way they solved the problems, explaining their thinking along the way.

The mathematical problem-solving process is both a mathematical and literacy process. To teach students how best to solve math word problems, insight into the process is helpful. The following six steps outline the basic problem-solving process and approaches for implementation (Adapted from Dacey and Collins 2012):

The Problem-Solving Process

1. Understand the problem.
- Read the problem.
- Clarify terms and concepts that are not understood.
- Ask: What is this problem asking?
- Decide: What information is relevant?

2. Make a plan.
- Consider: How will I solve this problem? Why?
- Consider: Are there other ways to solve this problem? What are they?
- Choose a strategy and make a specific plan to solve the problem.

3. Carry out the plan.
- Apply appropriate strategies and solve the problem.
- Ask: Do my approach and my answer make sense? Why or why not?

4. Check your answer.
- Ask: Did I answer the question that was being asked? If not, review question-answering strategies in Chapter 3.
- Ask: Is my arithmetic correct? (Check your work.)

5. Communicate and justify your thinking.
- Write a clear explanation that details your thinking process step-by-step.

6. Take it further.

- Solve the problem using a different strategy.
- Generalize based on your solution to the problem.
- Analyze how this problem is similar to or different from previous problems.
- Pose new and creative problems of your own.

After learning appropriate problem-solving strategies, students need sufficient practice and reinforcement. To fill this need, I suggest several books and series:

- *50 Leveled Math Problems, Level 3* by Linda Dacey and Anne Collins
- *Enrichment Units in Math, Grades 4–6* by Dianne Draze and Judy Leimbach
- *Family Math* by Jean Kerr Stenmark, Virginia Thompson, and Ruth Cossey
- *Out of The Labyrinth: Setting Mathematics Free* by Robert and Ellen Kaplan
- *Primarily Math: A Problem Solving Approach, Grades 2–4* by Sharon Eckert and Judy Leimbach
- *Think It, Show It Mathematics, Strategies for Explaining Thinking* by Gregory Denman

Using Radio Reading

Teachers know that the first step in the problem-solving process is to understand the problem. Radio Reading helps students tackle this first step in solving mathematical word problems. After students have read the problem independently, the teacher guides them through the following steps:

Radio Reading

1. Individual students reread the math word problem aloud as if they are broadcasting on the radio. They speak formally and project their voices so that everyone can hear them, including people sitting in the back of the room.

2. The students who are not reading close their books or cover their worksheets and listen carefully to the reader. Listeners concentrate on the meaning of the problem while they listen.

3. Students write down a summary of the problem. They refer to the text or worksheet if necessary.

4. Students ask themselves: What is the question asking? Then they write down what they think the question is asking.

5. Students turn to partners, share what they think the question is asking, and read their summaries to their partners.

6. After students have shared with partners, the teacher asks individuals to report to the class what they think the question is asking. The teacher then clears up any confusion about the problem's question.

7. Then the teacher encourages discussion about how to proceed to answer the question and solve the problem. After the class discusses various possible options, the teacher guides students, explaining the pros and cons of various approaches.

Using the Read Three Times Strategy

Solving mathematical word problems requires both solid math skills and strong reading comprehension ability. One way for teachers to help students improve their general reading comprehension as well as their math comprehension is to use the Read Three Times Strategy. This strategy has five steps:

Read Three Times Strategy

1. Students read the word problem quickly at first.

2. Students write a list of any words they do not understand. They can look up these words in the math text glossary or ask a peer or teacher for help.

3. Students then answer the following questions:

  - What is the problem asking me to do? How do I know?
  - What do I need to know?
  - What information, if any, is unnecessary?
  - What materials do I need?
  - What math operation(s) will I use? Why?

4. Students read through the problem at least two more times until they understand and can answer all the previous questions in step 3.

5. Students ask for help if they are stuck and do not understand how to proceed.

The Read Three Times Strategy is helpful in guiding students to consider each math problem carefully, take the time to think about it, and not give up when understanding is not instantaneous. In short, the Read Three Times approach helps students persevere in math and gives them a strategy to do so.

Planning Productive Mathematical Discussions

Classroom conversations are crucial to learning mathematics (Chapin, O'Connor, and Anderson 2009; Michaels, O'Connor and Resnick 2008). But how can teachers be most effective in presenting new math material and engaging students in productive mathematical discussions? *Five Practices for Orchestrating Productive Mathematical Discourse* by Mary Kay Stein and Margaret Schwan Smith (2011) sheds light on this challenge. This book addresses sensitive issues about how to conduct productive discussions in inquiry-based, student-centered math classrooms. The authors point out that productive discussions entail addressing students' inevitable misconceptions about math in respectful ways. They suggest a thoughtful, systematic five-part approach:

1. **Anticipate what students will do**; that is, think about what strategies they will likely use in solving a problem.

2. **Monitor students' work** in class while they approach the problem.

3. **Select students whose strategies merit discussion** with the whole class. For example, select student examples that will clarify the concept for other students or will address some commonly mistaken strategies for the particular type of math problem. (The teacher needs to use judgment about which strategies would be most helpful for the class, because some strategies selected by students might confuse others.)

4. **Have the selected students present their ideas** to the class, and sequence their presentations in ways that will increase learning and maximize understanding for the rest of the class. For example, a logical sequence would likely begin with a good first step for solving a mathematical word problem, followed by the second step, third step, and so forth. Depending on the needs and levels of the class, the teacher might suggest that different students present alternative approaches to the same problem, followed by discussion of the strengths and weaknesses of each alternative. The teacher should be encouraging to all the presenters and show genuine appreciation for their participation, while making sure to clarify the main math lesson.

5. **Connect the strategies presented** so that students understand the main math lessons.

Conclusion

By using creative math activities that combine interdisciplinary lessons in literacy with math, teachers can reach all types of students more successfully. Students with a complete range of math skills relate to these activities because the magnetic power of rhythm makes it as easy to remember a math concept as it is to recall a catchy tune. The power of rhythm and song embed math lessons deep in students' memories, reinforce daily lessons, and provide a pleasurable way to ensure lasting learning. By capitalizing on students' natural sense of rhythm and wonder, math teachers can instill in each student the skills, understanding, and attitudes that lead them to succeed and master math.

Reflect and Discuss

1. What math concepts in your curriculum would benefit from including rap, song, or poetry to help build conceptual or procedural understanding?

2. In what ways do you think your students would benefit from the strategies and activities described in this chapter?

3. How could you use journal writing in your next math lesson?

4. In what ways can you use the activities in this chapter to enhance students' vocabulary development?

Appendix A

References Cited

Allan, Nicole. 2013. "Who Will Tomorrow's Historians Consider Today's Greatest Innovators?" The Atlantic Magazine.

Allington, Richard L. 2009. "If They Don't Read Much…30 Years Later." In *Reading More, Reading Better*, edited by Elfrieda H. Hiebert, 30–54. New York, NY: Guildford.

Altieri, Jennifer L. 2011. *Content Counts! Developing Disciplinary Literacy Skills, K–6*. Newark, DE: The International Reading Association.

Ament, Alison. 2013. Personal Communication about Nerve Impulse Transmission, July 29.

Baines, Lawrence, and Anthony J. Kunkel, eds. 2000. *Going Bohemian: Activities That Engage Adolescents in the Art of Writing Well*. Newark, DE: The International Reading Association.

Bean, Rita M. 2009. *The Reading Specialist: Leadership for the Classroom, School, and Community*. New York, NY: Guilford.

Biancarosa, Gina, and Catherine E. Snow. 2006. *Reading Next: A Vision for Action and Research in Middle and High School Literacy*, A Report to the Carnegie Corporation of New York. New York, NY: Carnegie Corporation of New York.

Booth, Eric. 2009. *The Music Teaching Artist's Bible: Becoming a Virtuoso Educator*. London, UK: Oxford University Press.

Bouffard, Suzanne. 2014. "Using the Arts to Turn Schools Around." *Harvard Education Letter* 39 (2): 1–4. Cambridge, MA: Harvard Education Publishing Group.

Brice-Heath, Shirley. 1999. "Literacy and Social Practice." In *Literacy: An International Handbook*, edited by Daniel A. Wagner, Richard L. Venezsky, and Brian V. Street, 102–106. Boulder, CO: Westview Press.

Burks, Robert, Alex Heidenberg, Deann Leonni, and Tommy Ratliff. 2009. "Supporting the Motivators: A Faculty Development Issue." *PRIMUS* 19 (2): 127–145.

Catterall, James S., Susan A. Dumais, and Gillian Hampton-Thomas. 2012. "The Arts and Achievement in At-Risk Youth: Findings from Four Longitudinal Studies." Research Report # 55. Washington DC: National Endowment for the Arts.

Chall, Jeanne S. 1996. *Learning to Read: The Great Debate,* 2nd ed. New York, NY: McGraw-Hill.

Chard, David J., Sharon Vaughn, and Brenda-Jean Tyler. 2002. "A Synthesis of Research on Effective Interventions for Building Reading Fluency with Elementary Students with Learning Disabilities." *Journal of Learning Disabilities* 35 (5): 386–406.

Chapin, Suzanne H., Catherine O'Connor, and Nancy Canavan Anderson. 2009. *Classroom Conversations: Using Math Talk to Help Students Learn, Second Edition.* New York, NY: Scholastic.

Cleary, Brian. 2008. *The Action of Subtraction.* Minneapolis: MN: Lerner Publishing Group.

Cornell, Cathy. 1999. "I Hate Math! I Couldn't Learn It, and I Can't Teach It!" *Childhood Education* 75 (4): 225–230.

Costa, Arthur L., and Bena Rallick. 2008. *Learning and Leading with Habits of Mind: 16 Essential Characteristics for Success.* Alexandria, VA: Association for Supervision and Curriculum Development.

Craik, Fergus I. M., and Michael J. Watkins. 1973. "The Role of Rehearsal in Short-term Memory." *Journal of Verbal Learning and Verbal Behavior* 12 (6): 599–607.

Defeyter, Margaret Anne, Ricardo Russo, and Pamela Louise McPartlin. 2009. "The Picture Superiority Effect in Recognition Memory: A Developmental Study Using the Response Signal Procedure." *Cognitive Development* 24 (3): 265–273.

De Temple, Jeanne, and Catherine Elizabeth Snow. 1998. "Mother-Child Interactions Related to the Emergence of Literacy." In *Parenting Behavior in a Sample of Young Mothers in Poverty: Results of the New Chance Observational Study,* edited by Martha J. Zaslow and Carolyn A. Eldred, 114–169. New York, NY: Manpower Development Research Corporation.

Dewey, John. 1997. *How We Think: Reflective Practice, Journals and Learning Logs,* rev. ed. Boston, MA: DC Heath, Dover Reprint.

Dipple, Shannon. 2015. "Math Vocabulary Words." Primary Education Oasis. Accessed March 6. http://www.primary-education-oasis.com/math-vocabulary-words.html.

Donovan, Lisa, and Louise M. Pascale. 2012. *Integrating the Arts Across the Content Areas.* Huntington Beach, CA: Shell Education.

Drake, Susan M., and Rebecca C. Burns. 2004. *Meeting Standards through Integrated Curriculum.* Alexandria, VA: Association for Supervision and Curriculum Development.

Duke, Nell K. 2013. The Ninth Annual Jeanne S. Chall Memorial Lecture. Harvard Graduate School of Education, Cambridge, MA, October 9, 2013.

Duke, Nell K., Samantha Caughlin, Mary M. Juzwik, and Nicole M. Martin. 2011. *Reading and Writing Genre with Purpose in K–8 Classrooms.* Portsmouth, NH: Heinemann.

Duke, Nell K. and P. David Pearson. 2002. "Effective Practices for Developing Reading Comprehension." In *What Research Has to Say About Reading Comprehension,* 3rd edition, edited by S. Jay Samuels and Alan Farstrup, 3rd ed., 205–242, Newark, DE: International Reading Association.

Durica, Karen Morrow. 2007. *How We "Do" School: Poems to Encourage Teacher Reflection.* Newark, DE: The International Reading Association.

Dweck, Carol. 2008. *Mindset: The New Psychology of Success.* New York, NY: Ballantine Books.

Editorial. 2014. "Building Social Harmony, One Woodwind at a Time." *The Boston Globe.* December 7. http://www.bostonglobe.com/opinion/editorials/2014/12/07/massachusetts-cultural-council-pushes-sistema-music-education/0nNS1M9yCB9DNjpDUmg3xL/story.html.

Fink, Rosalie. 1996. "Successful Dyslexics: A Constructivist Study of Passionate Interest Reading." *Journal of Adolescent and Adult Literacy* 39 (4): 268–280.

———. 1998. "Literacy Development in Successful Men and Women with Dyslexia." *Annals of Dyslexia* 48: 311–346.

———. 2002. "Successful Careers: The Secrets of Adults with Dyslexia." *Career Planning and Adult Development Journal* 18 (1): 118–129.

———. 2003. "Reading Comprehension Struggles and Success: Case Study of a Leading Scientist." *The Primer* 31 (2): 19–30. Boston, MA: The Massachusetts Reading Association.

———. 2006. *Why Jane and John Couldn't Read—and How They Learned: A New Look at Striving Readers.* Newark, DE: The International Reading Association.

———. 2008. "High-Interest Reading Leaves No Child Behind," In *Inspiring Reading Success: Interest and Motivation in an Age of High-Stakes Testing,* edited by Rosalie Fink and S. Jay Samuels, 19–61. Newark, DE: International Reading Association.

———. 2012. "Read, Write, Rap, Rhyme." *The Newsletter of The New England Reading Association.*

———. 2016. "Rhythm and Rap Teach the Art of Argument." In *Learning Disabilities: A Contemporary Journal—Empowering Learners with Creative Arguments*, edited by Elena Grigorenko and Judith Randi.

Fink, Rosalie, and S. Jay Samuels, eds. 2008. *Inspiring Reading Success: Interest and Motivation in an Age of High-Stakes Testing.* Newark, DE: The International Reading Association.

Fink, Rosalie, Robert Wauhkonen, and Anne Pluto. 2012. "The Liberal Arts at Lesley College: Three Perspectives". In *A Century of Innovation: Lesley University,* edited by Cynthia Farr Brown and Michele Forinash, 146–167. Baltimore, MD: Publish America.

Fischer, Kurt W., and Maria Fusaro. 2008. "Using Student Interests to Motivate Learning." In *Inspiring Reading Success: Interest and Motivation in an Age of High-Stakes Testing,* edited by Rosalie Fink and S. Jay Samuels, 62–74. Newark, DE: International Reading Association.

Fisher, Douglas, and Nancy Frey. 2015. *Unstoppable Learning: Seven Essential Elements to Unleash Student Potential.* Bloomington, IN: Solution Tree Press.

Fiske, Edward B., ed. 1999. *Champions of Change: The Impact of the Arts on Learning.* Washington, DC: The Arts Education Partnership: The President's Committee on the Arts.

Foner, Philip S., 1950. *The Life and Writings of Frederick Douglass*, Vol. 2. New York, NY: International Publishers Company, Inc. http://www.pbs.org/wgbh/aia/part4/4h2927t.html.

Fredericks, Anthony D. 2011. "Building Literacy Bridges with Readers Theater." *School Library Monthly* 27 (4). http://www.schoollibrarymonthly.com/articles/FrederickS2011-v27n4p42.html.

Gardner, Howard. 1983. *Frames of Mind: The Theory of Multiple Intelligences*. New York, NY: Basic Books.

———. 2014. "Multiple Intelligences (MI) Theory: Implications for Teaching and Learning." The John T. Pratt Memorial Lecture. The Excellence in Special Education Summit. The Whitehead Institute for Biomedical Research, Massachusetts Institute of Technology. Cambridge, MA.

Gibas, Talia. 2012. "The Impact of the Arts on Learning." *Revisiting Research: Champions of Change* 23 (3).

Graves, Donald H. 1994. *A Fresh Look at Writing.* Portsmouth, NH: Heinemann.

Guthrie, John T., Susan Lutz Klauda, and Amy N. Ho. 2013. "Modeling the Relationships Among Reading Instruction, Motivation, Engagement, and Achievement for Adolescents." *Reading Research Quarterly* 48: 9–26.

Guthrie, John T., and Donna E. Alvermann. 1999. *Engaged Reading: Processes, Practices, and Policy Implications*. New York, NY: Teachers College Press.

Haltiwanger, Leigh and Amber M. Simpson. 2011. "Beyond the Write Answer: Mathematical Connections." Mathematics Teaching in the Middle School 18 (8): 492. Renton VA: The National Council of Teachers of Mathematics.

Harper, Rita, and Tom Bean. 2003. "Critical Literacy." Paper presented at The 47th Annual Convention of The International Reading Association, Orlando, FL, May 2003.

Hartman, Douglas K. 1997. *Doing Things with Texts: Mapping the Textual Practices of Two African American Male High School Students.* Report for The National Academy of Education And The Spencer Foundation.

Harvey, Stephanie. 2015. "Digging Deeper into Close Reading." *Reading Today* 32 (5): 30–31. Newark, DE: The International Reading Association.

Hendrick, George, and Willene Hendrick. 1996. *Selected Poems by Carl Sandburg.* Orlando: FL: Harcourt, Brace, Jovanovich.

Hiebert, Elfrieda H., and Michael L. Kamil. 2005. *Teaching and Learning Vocabulary: Bringing Research to Practice.* London: Lawrence Erlbaum Associates.

Hildebrandt, Carolyn, and Betty Zan. 2002. "Exploring the Art and Science of Musical Sound." In *Developing Constructivist Early Childhood Curriculum: Practical Principles and Activities*, edited by Rheta DeVries, Betty Zan, Carolyn Hildebrandt, Rebecca Edmiaston, and Christina Sales. New York, NY: Teachers College Press.

Hong Xu, Shelley. 2008. "Using Popular Culture Texts to Engage Students in Meaningful Literacy Learning." Paper presented at The Adelphi University 19th Annual Summer Literacy Institute. Garden City, NY. August 12.

Hong Xu, Shelley, Lark O. Zunich, and Rachel Sawyer Perkins. 2007. *Trading Cards to Comic Strips: Popular Culture Texts and Literacy Learning in Grades K–8.* Newark, DE: The International Reading Association.

Hughes, Langston. 1958. *The Langston Hughes Reader.* New York, NY: Brazilla, Inc.

Jackson, Carol D., and R. Jon Leffingwell. 1999. "The Role of Instructors in Creating Math Anxiety in Students from Kindergarten through College." *Mathematics Teacher* 92 (7): 583–587.

Jay-Z. 2010. "My President." *Decoded.* New York, NY: Random House.

Jensen, Eric. 2005. *Teaching with the Brain in Mind, 2nd Edition.* Alexandria, VA: Association for Supervision and Curriculum Development.

Johnson, Anne Frances. 2009. *Ecological Impacts of Climate Change.* Washington, DC: The National Academy of Science.

King, Hobart, and Angela king. 2015. "Teaching Plate Tectonics with Easy-to-Draw Illustrations." Geology.com. Accessed May 20. http://geology.com/nsta/.

Klingner, Janette K., Sharon Vaughn, Alison Gould Boardman, and Elizabeth A. Swanson. 2014. *How to Teach Collaborative Reading.* San Francisco, CA: Jossey-Bass.

Kucan, Linda. 2007. "'I' Poems: Invitations for Students to Deepen Literacy Understanding." *The Reading Teacher* 60: 518–525.

Lander, Jessica. 2015. "Teach Civics in School—But Do It Right." *The Boston Globe,* April 18. Op Ed, page A9.

Lawrence, Joshua F., Rebecca Givens Rolland, Lee Branum Mills, and Catherine E. Snow. 2014. "Generating Vocabulary Knowledge for At-Risk Middle School Readers: Contrasting Program Effects and Growth Trajectories." *Journal of Education for Students Placed At Risk (JESPAR)* 19 (2): 76-97.

Lesaux, Nonie. 2013. "Shifts in Practice to Promote Literacy Achievement in the Era of the Common Core State Standards." The Annual Jeanne S. Chall Memorial Lecture, Harvard Graduate School of Education, Cambridge, MA, October 9.

Lesley University Library. 2014. "Research Capstone." http://research.lesley.edy/ResearchCapstone.

Levpuscek, Melita Kuklek, and Maja Zupancic. 2009. "Math Achievement in Early Adolescence: The Role of Parental Involvement, Teachers' Behavior, and Students' Motivational Beliefs about Math." *Journal of Early Adolescence* (29) 4: 541–570.

Mancilla-Martinez, Jeanette, and Nonie K. Lesaux. 2011. "The Gap Between Spanish-Speakers' Word Reading and Word Knowledge: A Longitudinal Study." *Child Development* 82 (5) 1544–1560.

Marsh, Herbert W., and Rosalie O'Neill. 1984. "Self Description Questionnaire III: The Construct Validity of Multidimensional Self-Concept Ratings by Late Adolescents." *Journal of Educational Measurement* 21 (2): 153–174.

McMackin, Holly, and Mary McMackin. 2013. "Research, Decide, Teach." *The Primer* 41 (2): 2013–2014.

Michaels, Sarah, Catherine O'Connor, and Lauren Resnick. 2008. "Deliberative Discourse Idealized and Realized: Accountable Talk in the Classroom and in Civic Life." *Studies in Philosophy and Education* (27): 283–297.

Murray, Micah. 2015. "Behavioral Relevance of and Single-Trial Learning from Multisensory Processes." Multisensory Development, Plasticity, and Learning: From Basic to Clinical Science, Symposium of The Annual Meeting of the American Association for the Advancement of Science, San Jose, CA.

National Institute of Child Health and Human Development. 2000. *Report of the National Reading Panel: Teaching Children to Read: An Evidence-Based Assessment of the Scientific Research Literature and Its Implications for Reading Instruction* (NIH Publication No. 00-4769). Washington, DC: US Government Printing Office.

National Research Council. 2012. "A Framework for K–12 Science Education: Practices, Crosscutting Concepts, and Core Ideas." Washington DC. The National Academy of Science Press.

Next Generation Science Standards (NGSS) Lead States. 2013. "Next Generation Science Standards: By States, For States, Appendix—M: Connections to CCSS—Literacy in Science and Technical Subjects." Washington DC. www.nextgenscience.org.

Notorious B.I.G. 1994. "Juicy." *Ready to Die.* Big Poppa Music, Justin Publishing, Inc. and EMI April Music Inc.

Obama, Barack. 2010. *Of Thee I Sing: A Letter to My Daughters.* New York, NY: Alfred A. Knopf.

———. 2013. "Remarks by the President at Fourth of July Celebration." The White House. https://www.whitehouse.gov/the-press-office/2013/07/04/remarks-president-fourth-july-celebration.

Ortega, Nathanael. 2010. "Math Lesson Plan for 2nd Grade." www.lessonstudygroup.net.

Palmer, Charles Theodore H. 1847. "Try, Try Again." In *Poems*, edited by Emlen Franklin, Thomas Levingston Bayne, and Charles T.H. Palmer. New Haven, CT: J. H. Benham.

Paquette, Kelli R., and Sue A. Rieg. 2008. "Using Music to Support the Literacy Development of Young English Language Learners." *Early Childhood Education Journal* 36 (3): 227–232.

Pauk, Walter, and Ross J. Q. Owens. 2011. *How to Study in College.* Boston, MA: Houghton Mifflin.

Peebles, Jodi L. 2007. "Incorporating Movement with Fluency Instruction: A Motivation for Struggling Readers." *The Reading Teacher* 60 (6): 578–581.

Perret, Peter, and Janet Fox. 2006. *A Well-Tempered Mind: Using Music to Help Children Listen and Learn.* New York, NY: Dana Press.

Prosenjak, Nancy. 1999. "Reading Across the Grain of Gender." Paper presented at the Annual Meeting of The Colorado Council of The International Reading Association, Denver, CO.

Rasinski, Timothy. 2008. "Teaching Fluency Artfully." In *Inspiring Reading Success: Interest and Motivation in an Age of High-Stakes Testing*, edited by Rosalie Fink and S. Jay Samuels, 117–140. Newark, DE: International Reading Association.

Rasinski, Timothy, and S. Jay Samuels. 2011. "Reading Fluency: What It Is and What It Is Not." In *What Research Has to Say About Reading Instruction*, 4th ed., edited by S. Jay Samuels and Alan E. Farstrup, 94–114. Newark, DE: International Reading Association.

ReadWriteThink. 2015. "Analyzing Famous Speeches as Arguments." Accessed April 27, http://www.readwritethink.org/classroom-resources/lesson-plans/analyzing-famous-speeches-arguments-30526.html.

Renninger, K. Ann, and Suzanne E. Hidi (forthcoming). *The Power of Interest for Motivation and Engagement*. New York, NY: Routledge.

Renninger, K. Ann, Hidi, Suzanne E., and Andreas Krapp, eds. 1992. *The Role of Interest in Learning and Development*. Hillsdale, NJ: Erlbaum.

Rinne, Luke, Emma Gregory, Julia Yarmolinskyay, and Mariale Hardiman. 2011. "Why Arts Integration Improves Long-term Retention of Content." *Mind, Brain, and Education* 5 (2): 89–96.

Roe, Betty, and Sandy Smith. 2005. *Teaching Reading in Today's Middle Schools*, 95. Boston, MA: Houghton Mifflin.

Roe, Betty, Sandra H. Smith, and Paul C. Burns. 2011. *Teaching Reading in the Elementary Schools*, 11th edition. Boston, MA: Houghton Mifflin.

Rothstein, Dan and Luz Santana. 2011. *Make Just One Change: Teach Students to Ask Their Own Questions*. Cambridge, MA: Harvard Education Press.

Samuels, S. Jay. 2006. "Toward a Model of Reading Fluency." In *What Research Has to Say About Fluency Instruction*, edited by S. Jay Samuels and Alan E. Farstrup, 24–46. Neward, DE: International Reading Association.

Seeger, Pete. 2004. "Introduction." In *Rise Up Singing: The Group Singing Songbook,* edited by Peter Blood and Annie Patterson, 15th ed. Bethlehem, PA: The Sing Out Corporation.

Shanahan, Timothy. 2006. *The National Reading Panel Report.* Naperville, IL: Learning Point Associates.

———. 2012. "What Is Close Reading?" Shanahan On Literacy. http://www.shanahanonliteracy.com/2012/06what-is-close-reading.html.

Silverman, Michael J. 2010. "The Effect of Pitch, Rhythm, and Familiarity on Working Memory and Anxiety as Measured by Digit Recall Performance." *Journal of Music Therapy* 47 (1): 70–83.

Simpson, Eileen B. 1979. *Reversals: A Personal Account of Victory Over Dyslexia*. Boston, MA: Houghton Mifflin.

Sitomer, Alan Lawrence, and Michael Cirelli. 2004. *Hip-Hop Poetry and the Classics*. Beverly Hills, CA: Milk Mug.

Snow, Catherine E. 2002. "Reading for Understanding: Toward a Research and Development Program in Reading Comprehension." Santa Monica, CA: RAND Corporation. www.rand.org.

———. 2010. "Academic Language and the Challenge of Reading for Learning About Science." *Science*. Washington DC: The National Academy of Sciences and The American Association for the Advancement of Science.

Snow, Catherine E., M. Susan Burns, and Peg Griffin, eds. 1998. *Preventing Reading Difficulties in Young Children*. Washington, DC: National Academy Press.

Snow, Catherine E., Joshua F. Lawrence, and Claire White. 2009. "Generating Knowledge of a Language Among Urban Middle School Students." *Journal of Research on Educational Effectiveness* 2 (4): 325–344.

Sousa, David A., ed. 2010. *Mind, Brain, and Education: Neuroscience Implications for the Classroom*. Bloomington, IN: Solution Tree Press.

Sousa, David A. 2011. "Mind, Brain, and Education: The Impact of Educational Neuroscience on the Science of Teaching." In *Mind, Brain, and Education: Implications for Educators*, edited by Lynn Butler-Kisber, 5 (1): 37–44.

Strickland, Dorothy. 2011. *Teaching Phonics Today: Word Study Strategies through the Grades,* Second Edition. Newark, DE: International Reading Association.

Stier, Catherine. 2004. If I were President. Park Ridge, IL: Albert Whitman Company.

Tamer, Mary. 2015. "Word Generation at Work: Building Vocabulary Via Word Generation Helps NYC Students Enhance their Debate Skills." Usable Knowledge: Connecting Research to Practice. https://www.gse.harvard.edu/news/uk/15/02/word-generation-work.

Teague, P. Terrett, and George G. Austin-Martin. 1981. "Effects of a Mathematics Methods Course on Prospective Elementary School Teachers' Math Attitudes, Math Anxiety, and Teaching Performance." Paper presented at the Annual Meeting of the Southwest Educational Research Association. Dallas, TX. February 1981.

Tough, Paul. 2012. *How Children Succeed*. Boston, MA: Houghton Mifflin Harcourt.

US Department of Education. 2014. "Program Description." http://ww2. ed.gov/programs/readingfirst/index.html

Wanzek, Jeanne, Sharon Vaughn, Shawn C. Kent, Elizabeth A. Swanson, Greg Roberts, Martha Haynes, Anna-Mária Fall, Stephanie J. Stillman-Spisak, and Michael Solis. 2014. "The Effects of Team-Based Learning on Social Studies Knowledge Acquisition in High School." *Journal of Research on Educational Effectiveness* 7 (2): 183–204.

Werner, Emmy, and Ruth Smith. 1992. *Overcoming the Odds: High Risk Children from Birth to Adulthood.* New York, NY: Cornell University Press. Wiley, Kathleen. "The Prime Numbers Rap."

Wilhelm, Jeffrey D. 2002. *Action Strategies for Deepening Comprehension.* New York, NY: Scholastic.

Winner, Ellen. 1996. *Gifted Children: Myths and Realities.* New York, NY: Basic Books.

Wise, Julie B., and Alexandra Panos. 2014. "Going Digital in the Social Studies Classroom with Evidence-Based Argumentation." *Journal of Adolescent and Adult Literacy.* Newark, DE: International Reading Association.

Wolf, Maryanne. 2008. *Proust and the Squid: The Story and Science of the Reading Brain.* New York, NY: HarperCollins.

Wolfman, Ira. 2002. *Climbing Your Family Tree: Online and Off-line Genealogy for Kids.* New York, NY: Workman Publishing.

Yenawine, Philip. 2013. *Visual Thinking Strategies: Using Art to Deepen Learning across School Disciplines.* Cambridge, MA: Harvard Education Press.

Appendix B

Additional Raps, Songs, and Poems

The Parts of Speech Song

by Rosalie Fink

(Sung to the tune of "Frere Jacques")

Nouns are persons,
Nouns are places,
Nouns are things,
Nouns are things.

Mother, father, teacher,
Car, house, or computer,
These are nouns.
These are nouns.

Adjectives
Describe somebody
Or something,
Or something.

Lumpy, soft, or ugly,
Short or tall or messy,
Are adjectives.
They describe a noun.

Verbs show action,
Verbs show action,
Yes they do,
Yes they do.

Run, jump, shout, and swim,
Whisper, write, or dance,
These are verbs,
They're action words.

Adverbs tell HOW
Things are done.
They modify verbs,
They end in "ly."

Modestly and greedily,
Stupidly and sleepily,
Are all adverbs,
They modify verbs.

Exclamations
Show emotions,
Like surprise,
And silly sounds.

Wow! Yuk! Ouch! And Awesome!
These are exclamations,
So use an ex-
clamation mark!

Scientists Use Observation Rap

by Rosalie Fink

Verse 1

Scientists use observation
Record their findings
And conduct investigations.
Based on the evidence
That they see
They make explanations
And draw conclusions.

Chorus

Evidence changes scientists' conclusions
Evidence prevents them from having false illusions.
The story of science is always changing
Based on observation and discovery.

Verse 2
When two scientists disagree,
They do more experiments
And analyze the evidence.
When two scientists disagree
They experiment more and
Change science history.

Chorus

●●●

The Climate Change Song

by Rosalie Fink
(Sung to the tune of "Jingle Bells")

Climate change, climate change,
It's very much with us.
The Earth is getting warmer
And life is getting tough.

But we can do a lot to help
And slow the warming, hey!
Reduce our carbon imprint;
Use alternative energy!

●●●

What Happened to Poor Pluto? Rap

by Rosalie Fink

Nine planets used to be the rule
But now there are only eight.
That is what they teach in school,
What sealed poor Pluto's fate?

New telescopes showed Pluto's size
And charted its orbit in this mission.
Scientists peering in the skies
Changed their definition.

A planet must be big to fit
And own its circle 'round the sun
But Pluto's small and its orbit
Crosses Neptune's on its run.

Now listen up 'bout Pluto's fate
There is no need to fret.
Though no longer in the big eight,
It's now a dwarf planet.

Fairness for All

by Rosalie Fink

(Sung to the tune of "London Bridge Is Falling Down")

Gloria takes music lessons,
Music lessons, music lessons,
Her school has the money for
Music instruments.

Rosa wants the lessons too,
Lessons too, lessons too,
But her school lacks money for
Music instruments.

The girls talk to the Booster Club,
Booster Club, Booster Club,
The Booster Club votes to
Share their money.

Now each school has the money for,
Money for, money for,
Now each school has the money for
Music instruments.

Now everyone can study music,
Study music, study music,
Now everyone can study music
If they want to.

I Can't Get No Little Fractions*

by Dona Herweck Rice
(Sung to the tune of "I Can't Get No Satisfaction")

I can't get no little fractions,
I can't get no little fractions,
If I use and I use and I use and I use
Just whole numbers, just whole numbers.

'Cause a fraction is a part
Of a number that is whole.
It has a numerator up top
And a denominator below.
It's just a part of a whole, so
I can't get no little fractions
If I use just whole numbers.

I can't get no little fractions,
I can't get no little fractions,
If I use and I use and I use and I use
Just whole numbers, just whole numbers.

When I'm eatin' my pizza
And my mom comes out to tell me
I have to share it equally,
But I can't share it 'cause it's only one,
She says to use fractions instead.
I can't get no little fractions.
If I use just whole numbers.

I can't get no little fractions,
I can't get no little fractions,
If I use and I use and I use and I use
Just whole numbers, just whole numbers.

I can't get no, I can't get no,
I can't get no little fractions,
No little fractions, no little fractions, no little fractions!

Money Counts Rap*

by Lisa Zamosky

One, two, three four five.
Money counts, it's no jive!
A dollar buys a red balloon
Or candy if you like,
But if you keep on saving,
You could buy a brand new bike!
Four quarters make a dollar bill,
One hundred pennies, too.
But if you saved a million...
Just think what you could do!

• •

Divide with Fractions Rap*

by Millie Kateman

To divide with fractions,
Don't be shy.
Just flip the second
And multiply.
Use the reciprocal (*clap, clap, clap*)
Use the reciprocal (*clap, clap, clap*)

• •

My Tools to Measure*

by Dona Herweck Rice

How long? How fast? How far? How wide?
It isn't hard to do
If I use my instruments—
I'll show you what to do!

If I want to measure
Length or width or height,
I'll find myself a ruler
To measure it just right.

If I want to measure
Ingredients for a cake,
I'll use cups and spoons for volume
Before I let it bake.

If I want to measure
How much it is I weigh,
I'll stand quite still upon the scale
And read what the numbers say

If I want to measure
The temperature today,
I'll read our thermometer
Then go outside to play.

If I want to measure
How quickly I can run,
I'll time it with a stopwatch
To see what I have done.

If I want to measure
The distance that we go,
I'll read the odometer
To learn what I should know.

I know that I can measure
Weight and speed and size.
Then I can measure the pride I feel
By the twinkle in my eyes!

• •

Number Cheer*

by Dona Herweck Rice

Teacher: One, one, can I hear a one?
    All: One!
Teacher: Let's Hear it for one!
    All: One me, one you, one Earth, one sun,
        One, one, one!
Teacher: Two, two, can I hear a two?
    All: Two!
Teacher: Let's hear it for two!
    All: Two eyes, two ears, two socks, two shoes,
        Two, two, two!

Teacher: Three, three, can I hear a three?

    All: Three!

Teacher: Let's Hear it for three!

    All: Three blocks, three bikes, three birds, three bees, Three, three, three!

Teacher: Four, four, can I hear a four?

    All: Four!

Teacher: Let's Hear it for four!

    All: Four days, four nights, four less, four more, Four, four, four!

Teacher: Five, five, can I hear a five?

    All: Five!

Teacher: Let's Hear it for five!

    All: Five balls, five bats, five swings, five slides, Five, five, five!

Teacher: Five, five, can I hear a five?

    All: Five!

Teacher: Let's Hear it for five! Five, five, five!

I'm Positive About Negatives*

by Dona Herweck Rice

Mama says positivity is best
And I'm positive she's right.
But Teacher said, "Study negatives,"
And I think that I just might!

Each number has absolute value,
Whether it's a low value or a lot.
And each number has a sign
Whether you see it there or not.

The numbers you learned in preschool
Are positive as can be
They have a value you can count on
Such as 8, 12, or 53.

A + sign may mark a positive,
Or it might be written on its own.
Either way its value is clear
And there's nothing more to be known.

A negative is quite different
Though it too has a value that's clear.
A - sign marks the negative,
So you can spot it, never fear.

To understand positives and negatives
Think of numbers in a line.
A zero marks the middle
And a 1 lines up on either side.

But the 1 on the right is a positive
And it's followed by 2, 3, and 4,
And the 1 on the left is a negative
And the 2, 3, and 4 come before.

When adding together positives
Or when adding negatives too,
Add only the absolute values
And keep the positive or negative view.

BUT…if adding a positive and negative
The negative changes the action,
And instead of addition
It seems like you do subtraction.

And if you subtract a negative,
Subtraction plus the negative sign
Make the answer a positive
(Which kind of blows your mind!)

Negatives are tricky business!
They seem to play a confusing game,
But when you know how to handle them
They become quite steady and tame.

So watch out for clever negatives
Hanging out with their positive friends,
And stay positive about your negatives
So you can manage them all in the end!

The Pi Rap*
by Rosalie Fink

Verse 1
Pi is a constant
Three point one four,
It's always the same
And that's for sure.

Chorus

The circumference divided by the diameter
That's the ratio of C to D,
Always remains the same.
It's no mystery!

Verse 2
If a circle is big
Or even if it's small,
Pi remains the same
Three point one four for all.

Chorus

Verse 3
Pi shows the ratio of
C to D.
Why it's always the same
It's no mystery.

Chorus

*These raps and songs should only be introduced once students have solid conceptual understanding of the mathematical concepts.

230

Appendix C

Resources

Literacy Resources

Ahlberg, Janet, and Allan Ahlberg. 1986. *The Jolly Postman or Other People's Letters*. New York, NY: William Heineman.

Allan, Karen Kuelthau, and Margery Staman Miller. 2005. *Literacy and Learning in the Content Areas: Strategies for Middle and Secondary School Teachers,* 2nd ed. Boston, MA: Cengage Learning.

Beaty, Andrea. 2013. *Rosie Revere, Engineer*. New York, NY: Abrams Books for Young Readers.

Berger, Barbara Helen. 2000. *A Lot of Otters*, reprint ed. New York, NY: Puffin Books.

Bingham, Kelly. 2012. *Z Is for Moose*. New York, NY: Greenwillow Books.

Boynton, Sandra. 1993. *Barnyard Dance!* New York, NY: Workman Publishing Company.

Brozo, William G., Gary Moorman, and Carla K. Meyer. 2014. *Wham! Teaching with Graphic Novels across the Curriculum*. New York, NY: Teachers College Press.

Buss, Kathleen, and Leslie McClain-Ruelle, eds. 2000. *Creating a Classroom Newspaper*. Newark, DE: International Reading Association.

Cabatingan, Erin, and Matthew Myers. 2012. *A Is for Musk Ox*. New York, NY: Roaring Book Press.

Calkins, Lucy McCormick. 1994. *The Art of Teaching Writing*. Portsmouth, NH: Heinemann.

Cappiello, Mary Ann, and Erika Thulin Dawes. 2013. *Teaching with Text Sets.* Huntington Beach, CA: Shell Education.

Davis, Judy, and Sharon Hill. 2003. *The No-nonsense Guide to Teaching Writing: Strategies, Structures, and Solutions.* Portsmouth, NH: Heinemann.

Degen, Bruce. 1995. *Jamberry.* New York, NY: HarperFestival.

Dyer, Jane. 1998. *Animal Crackers: Nursery Rhymes.* New York, NY: Little, Brown Books for Young Readers.

Fletcher, Ralph. 2004. *Poetry Matters: Writing a Poem from the Inside Out.* South Hadley, MA: Arrowpoint.

Gaiman, Neil. 2009. *Crazy Hair.* New York, NY: HarperCollins.

Grossman, Virginia, and Sylvia Long. 1991. *Ten Little Rabbits.* San Francisco, CA: Chronicle Books.

Guarino, Deborah. 1989. *Is Your Mama a Llama?* New York, NY: Scholastic Press.

Gutiérrez, Peter. 2014. *The Power of Scriptwriting! Teaching Essential Writing Skills through Podcasts, Graphic Novels, Movies, and More.* New York, NY: Teachers College Press.

Heard, Georgia. 1989. *For the Good of the Earth and Sun: Teaching Poetry.* Portsmouth, NH: Heinemann.

Hiebert, Elfrieda. 2015. "What's Complex in Text Complexity?" Reading Today, 31 (2): 18–19. Newark, DE: International Reading Association.

Iadonisi, Carmin, and Amanda Word. 2015. *Whiny Whiny Rhino.* Auburn, ME: Blue Blanket Publishing.

Ippolito, Jacy, Joshua Fahey Lawrence, and Colleen Zaller, eds. 2013. *Adolescent Literacy in the Era of the Common Core: From Research into Practice.* Cambridge, MA: Harvard Education Press.

Kane, Sharon. 2007. *Integrating Literature in the Content Areas.* Scottsdale, AZ: Holcomb Hathaway Publishers.

Karchmer-Klein, Rachel, and Valerie Shinas. 2012. "Guiding Principles for Supporting New Literacies in Your Classroom." *The Reading Teacher 65* (5): 285–290.

Lane, Barry. 1993. *After the End: Teaching and Learning Creative Revision.* Portsmouth, NH: Heinemann.

Lapp, Diane. 2013. *Teaching Students to Closely Read Texts: How and When?* Newark, DE: International Reading Association.

Leu, Donald J. Jr., Deborah Diadiun Leu, and Julie Coiro. 2004. *Teaching with the Internet K–12: New Literacies for New Times.* Norwood, MA: Christopher-Gordon Publishers, Inc.

MacLachlan, Patricia. 1996. *Sarah, Plain and Tall.* New York, NY: Scholastic.

Marx, Pamela. 1997. *Take a Quick Bow!* Tuscon, AZ: Good Year Books.

McPhillips, Shirley. 2014. *Poem Central: Word Journeys with Readers and Writers.* Stenhouse Publishers.

Patricelli, Leslie. 2003. *Quiet Loud.* Somerville, MA: Candlewick Press.

Rakoncay, Melinda. 1987. *Hop Like a Bunny! Waddle Like a Duck!* Racine, WI: Western Publishing Company.

Rey, H.A. 1998. *Curious George's ABCs.* New York, NY: Houghton Mifflin Company.

Robb, Laura. 1999. *Brighten Up Boring Beginnings and Other Quick Writing Lessons.* New York, NY: Scholastic.

Romain, Trevor. 1997. *Bullies Are a Pain in the Brain.* Minneapolis, MN: Free Spirit Publishing.

Dr. Seuss. 1957. *The Cat in the Hat.* New York, NY: Random House.

———. 1958. *The Cat in the Hat Comes Back.* New York, NY: Random House.

———. 1960. *Green Eggs and Ham.* New York, NY: Dr. Random House.

Vamos, Samantha R. 2013. *Alphabet Trucks.* Watertown, MA: Charlesbridge.

Willard, Nancy. 1991. *Pish, Posh, Said Hieronymus Bosch.* New York, NY: Harcourt Brace & Company.

Zambo, Debby, and William G. Brozo. 2009. *Bright Beginnings for Boys: Engaging Young Boys in Active Literacy.* Newark, DE: International Reading Association.

Reader's Theater

Blank, Carla, and Jody Roberts. 1996. *Live on Stage: Teacher Resource Book, Performing Arts for Middle School.* New York, NY: Dale Seymour Publications.

Feyder, Linda, ed. 1992. *Shattering the Myth: Plays by Hispanic Women.* Houston, TX: Arte Publico Press.

Fredericks, Anthony D. 2001. *Silly Salamanders and Other Slightly Stupid Stuff for Readers Theatre.* Englewood, CO: Teacher Ideas Press.

Jenkins, Diana R. 2004. *Just Deal with It! Funny Readers Theatre for Life's Not-So-Funny Moments.* Englewood, CO: Teacher Ideas Press.

Laughlin, Mildred Knight, and Kathy Howard Latrobe. 1989. *Readers Theatre for Children: Scripts and Script Development.* Englewood, CO: Teacher Ideas Press.

————. 1998. *Readers Theatre for Young Adults: Scripts and Script Development.* Englewood, CO: Teacher Ideas Press.

Laughlin, Mildred Knight, Peggy Tubbs Black, and Margery Kirby Loberg. 1991. *Social Studies Readers Theatre for Children: Scripts and Script Development.* Englewood, CO: Teacher Ideas Press.

Marx, Pamela. 1997. *Take a Quick Bow: 26 Short Plays for Classroom Fun.* Culver City, CA: Good Year Books.

Talbot, Ann R. 1994. *The Lost Cat: and Other Primary Plays for Oral Reading.* Billerica, MA: Curriculum Associates.

Wolfman, Judy. 2004. *How and Why Stories for Reader's Theatre.* Englewood, CO: Teacher Ideas Press.

Worthy, Jo. 2005. *Readers Theater for Building Fluency: Stategies and Scripts for Making the Most of This Highly Effective, Motivating, and Research-Based Approach to Oral Reading.* Bethesda, MD: Teaching Strategies.

Poetry

Bernier-Grand, Carmen T. 2004. *Cesar: Sí, Se Puede! Yes, We can!* Tarrytown, NY: Marshall Cavendish.

Curtis, Carolyn. 2004. *I Took the Moon for a Walk*. Cambridge, MA: Barefoot Books.

Hopkins, Lee Bennett. 1999. *Lives: Poems About Famous Americans*. New York, NY: HarperCollins.

Hughes, Langston. 1951. "Harlem: A Dream Deferred." *Montage of a Dream Deferred*. Austin, TX: Holt, Rinehart, and Winston.

Kleinberg, Naomi. 2012. *Elmo's Rockin' Rhyme Time!* New York, NY: Random House Children's Books.

Koch, Kenneth, and Kate Farrell, eds. 1985. *Talking to the Sun: An Illustrated Anthology of Poems for Young People*. New York, NY: Henry Holt and Co.

Medina, Tony. 2002. *Love to Langston*. New York, NY: Lee & Low.

Mora, Pat. 2000. *My Own True Name: New and Selected Poems for Young Adults*. Houston, TX: Arte Publico.

Nye, Naomi Shihab. 2002. *19 Varieties of Gazelle: Poems of the Middle East*. New York, NY: Greenwillow Books.

Panzer, Nora. ed. 1994. *Celebrate America in Poetry and Art*. New York, NY: Hyperion Books for Children.

Sword, Elizabeth Hauge, ed. 1995. *A Child's Anthology of Poetry*. New York, NY: HarperCollins Publishers.

Williams, Vera B. 2001. *Amber Was Brave, Essie Was Smart*. New York, NY: Greenwillow Books.

Wood, Julie M. 2004. *Literacy Online: New Tools for Struggling Readers and Writers*. Cambridge, MA: Harvard Education Press.

———. 2014. *CyberKids: Struggling Readers and Writers and How Computers Can Help*. Portsmouth, NH: Heinemann.

Literature Resources

Angelou, Maya. 1970. *I Know Why the Caged Bird Sings*. New York, NY: Random House.

Cook, Karin. 1997. *What Girls Learn: A Novel*. New York, NY: Vintage Books.

Krakauer, Jon. 1997. *Into the Wild*. New York, NY: Random House.

Lima, Carolyn W., and John A. Lima. 2006. *A to Zoo: Subject Access to Children's Picture Books*, 7th ed. Westport, CT: Libraries Unlimited.

Obama, Barack. 2004. *Dreams from My Father: A Story of Race and Inheritance*. New York, NY: Three Rivers Press.

Odean, Kathleen. 1997. *Great Books for Boys: More than 600 Books for Boys 2–14*. New York, NY: Ballantine.

————. 1997. *Great Books for Girls: More than 600 Books to Inspire Today's Girls and Tomorrow's Women*. New York, NY: Ballantine.

Silvey, Anita. 2004. *100 Best Books for Children*. New York, NY: Houghton Mifflin Company.

Wedwick, Linda, and Jessica Ann Wutz. 2008. *Bookmatch: How to Scaffold Student Book Selection for Independent Reading*. Newark, DE: International Reading Association.

Yolen, Jane, and Heidi E. Y. Stemple. 2009. *Fairy Tale Feasts: A Literary Cookbook for Young Readers and Eaters*. Northampton, MA: Crocodile Books, USA.

Math Resources

Adler, David A. 1996. *Fraction Fun*. New York, NY: Holiday House Press.

Burns, Marilyn. 1994. *The Greedy Triangle*. New York, NY: Scholastic.

Cleary, Brian P. 2006. *The Action of Subtraction*. Minneapolis, MN: Millbrook Press.

Dacey, Linda, and Anne Collins. 2012. *50 Leveled Math Problems, Level 3*. Huntington Beach, CA: Shell Education.

Denman, Gregory A. 2013. *Think It, Show It Mathematics: Strategies for Explaining Thinking*. Huntington Beach, CA: Shell Education.

Draze, Dianne, and Judy Leimbach. 1995. *Enrichment Units in Math, Grades 4–6.* San Luis Obispo, CA: Dandy Lion Publications.

Eckert, Sharon, and Judy Leimbach. 1993. *Primarily Math: A Problem Solving Approach, Grades 2–4.* San Luis Obispo, CA: Dandy Lion Publications.

Enzensberger, Hans Magnus. 2010. *The Number Devil: A Mathematical Adventure.* New York, NY: St. Martin's Press.

Flannery, Sarah, and David Flannery. 2001. *In Code: A Mathematical Journey.* New York, NY: Workman Publishing.

Heligman, Deborah. 2013. *The Boy Who Loved Math: The Improbable Life of Paul Erdos.* New York: Roaring Brook Press.

Kaplan, Robert, and Ellen Kaplan. 2007. *Out of the Labyrinth: Setting Mathematics Free.* London: Oxford University Press.

Marshall, Jason. 2012. *The Math Dude's Quick and Dirty Guide to Algebra.* New York, NY: Macmillan.

McKellar, Danica. 2007. *Math Doesn't Suck.* New York, NY: Penguin.

Pappas, Theoni. 2007. *The Adventures of Penrose, the Mathematical Cat.* San Carlos, CA: Wide World Publishing/Tetra.

———. 2008. *Math Talk: Mathematical Ideas in Poems for Two Voices.* San Carlos, CA: Wide World Publishing/Tetra.

———. 2009. *Fractals, Googols, and Other Mathematical Tales.* San Carlos, CA: Wide World Publishing/Tetra.

———. 2011. *Math for Kids and Other People Too!* San Carlos, CA: Wide World Publishing/Tetra.

Rey, H. A. 2005. *Curious George Learns to Count from 1 to 100: Counting, Grouping, Mapping, and More!* Boston: Houghton Mifflin Harcourt.

Schwartz, David M. 1985. *How Much Is a Million?* New York, NY: William Morrow & Co.

Scieszka, Jon. 2010. *Math Curse.* New York, NY: Scholastic.

Stein, Mary Kay, and Margaret S. Smith. 2011. *Five Practices for Orchestrating Productive Mathematical Discourse.* Thousand Oaks, CA: Corwin.

Stenmark, Jean Kerr, Virginia Thompson, and Ruth Cossey. 1986. *Family Math*. Berkeley, CA: The University of California.

Tang, Greg. 2001. *The Grapes of Math*. New York, NY: Scholastic.

Science Resources

Aguilar, David A. 2011. *13 Planets: The Latest View of the Solar System*. Washington, DC: National Geographic.

Ardley, Neil. 1991. *The Science Book of Electricity*. San Diego, CA: Harcourt Children's Books.

Baldwin, Robert F. 1998. *This Is the Sea That Feeds Us*. Nevada City, CA: Dawn Publications.

Balkwill, Fran, and Mic Rolph. 2002. *Enjoy Your Cells*. Cold Spring Harbor, NY: Cold Spring Harbor Laboratory Press.

———. 2002. *Germ Zappers*. New York, NY: Cold Spring Harbor Laboratory Press.

———. 2002. *Have a Nice DNA*. Cold Spring Harbor, NY: Cold Spring Harbor Laboratory Press.

Barber, Jacqueline. 2007. *Jess Makes Hair Gel*. Nashua, New Hampshire: Delta Education.

Bell, Trudy E. 2008. *Earth's Journey through Space*. New York, NY: Chelsea House Publishers.

Bortz, Fred. 1995. *Catastrophe! Great Engineering Failure—and Success*. New York, NY: W. H. Freeman & Co.

Cervetti, Gina. 2010. *Why Do Scientists Disagree?* Nashua, New Hampshire: Delta Education.

Connolly, Sean. 2008. *The Book of Totally Irresponsible Science: 64 Daring Experiments for Young Scientists*. New York, NY: Workman Publishing Company, Inc.

Denman, Gregory A. 2013. *Think It, Show It Science: Strategies for Demonstrating Knowledge*. Huntington Beach, CA: Shell Education.

Harbaugh, Kathy. 2002. *Middle School Science Challenge*. Arlington, VA: National Science Teachers Association.

Kudlinski, Kathleen V. 2008. *Boy, Were We Wrong About the Solar System!* New York, NY: Dutton Children's Books.

Macaulay, David. 1998. *The New Way Things Work: From Levers to Lasers, Windmills to Websites.* Boston, MA: Houghton Mifflin.

Popey, David. 2009. *Perplexing Perceptions: Over 125 Challenging Exercises.* San Diego, CA: Thunder Bay Press.

Rose, Steven, and Alexander Lichtenfels. 1997. *Brainbox.* London, England: Portland Press, Limited.

Scieszka, Jon. 2004. *Science Verse.* New York, NY: Penguin Young Readers.

Stewart, Melissa. 2006. *A Place for Butterflies.* Atlanta, GA: Peachtree Publishers, Ltd.

Stille, Darlene R. 1995. *Extraordinary Women Scientists.* New York, NY: Children's Press.

VanCleave, Janice. 2001. *Teaching the Fun of Science.* New York, NY: John Wiley & Sons, Inc.

Wiese, Jim. 2002. *Sports Science: 40 Goal-scoring, High-flying, Medal-winning Experiments for Kids!* Hoboken, NJ: John Wiley & Sons, Inc.

Wolfman, Ira. 2002. *Climbing Your Family Tree: Online and Off-line Genealogy for Kids.* New York, NY: Workman Publishing.

Social Studies Resources

Adler, David. 1994. *A Picture Book of George Washington.* New York, NY: Scholastic.

Adler, David. 1994. *A Picture Book of Helen Keller.* New York, NY: Scholastic.

———. 1996. *The Dial Book of Animal Tales from around the World.* New York, NY: Dial.

Ahmedi, Farah, with Tamin Ansary. 2005. *The Story of My life: An Afghan Girl on the Other Side of the Sky.* New York, NY: Simon & Schuster.

Bingham, Jane. 2005. *African Art and Culture.* Chicago, IL: Heinemann-Raintree.

Blood, Peter, and Annie Patterson, Eds. 2004. *Rise Up Singing: The Group Singing Songbook.* Bethlehem, PA: Sing Out!

Brallier, Jess. 2002. *Who Was Albert Einstein?* New York, NY: Grosset & Dunlap.

Coleman, Penny. 1992. *Spies! Women in the Civil War.* New York, NY: Shoe Tree Press.

Coles, Robert. 1995. *The Story of Ruby Bridges.* New York, NY: Scholastic.

Cooper, Floyd. 1996. *Mandela: From the Life of the South African Statesman.* New York, NY: Philomel Books.

Copley, Robert. 2000. *The Tall Mexican: The Life of Hank Aguirre, All-star Pitcher, Businessman, Humanitarian.* Houston, TX; Arte Público Press.

Falk, Laine. 2009. *Meet President Barack Obama.* New York, NY: Scholastic.

Foner, Nancy. 2000. *From Ellis Island to JFK: New York's Two Great Waves of Immigration.* New Haven, CT: Yale University Press.

Gaff, Jackie. 2004. *Excavating the Past: Ancient Egypt.* Chicago, IL: Heinemann-Raintree.

Hatt, Christine. 2004. *Excavating the Past: Greece.* Chicago, IL: Heinemann-Raintree.

———. 2004. *Excavating the Past: The Viking World.* Chicago, IL: Heinemann-Raintree.

Heligman, Deborah. 2003. *High Hopes: A Photobiography of John F. Kennedy.* Washington DC: National Geographic.

Katz, Bobbi. 2000. *We the People.* New York, NY: HarperCollins.

Khanduri, Kamini. 2003. *Japanese Art and Culture.* Chicago, IL: Heinemann-Raintree.

Keller, Bill, and Jill Abramson. 2009. *Obama: The Historic Journey.* New York, NY: Calaway.

Lewis, Elizabeth. 2003. *Mexican Art and Culture.* Chicago, IL: Heinemann-Raintree.

MacDonald, Fiona. 2005. *Excavating the Past: Ancient Rome.* Chicago, IL: Heinemann-Raintree.

MacDonald, Margaret Read. 1992. *Peace Tales: World Folktales to Talk About.* Hamden, CT: Linnet Books.

Malone, Mary. 1995. *Maya Lin: Architect and Artist*. New York, NY: Enslow Publishers.

Mayo, Margaret. 1993. *Magical Tales from Many Lands*. New York, NY: Dutton.

McMane, Fred, and Catherine Wolf. 1995. *Winning Women: Eight Great Athletes and Their Unbeatable Stories*. New York, NY: Bantam.

Obama, Barack. 2010. *Of Thee I Sing: A Letter to My Daughters.* New York, NY: Alfred A. Knopf.

Rappaport, Doreen. 2001. *Martin's Big Words: The Life of Dr. Martin Luther King, Jr.* New York, NY: Disney-Hyperion.

Rockwell, Anne. 2002. *Only Passing Through: The Story of Sojourner Truth.* New York, NY: Dragonfly Books.

Ryan, Pam Muñoz. 2002. *When Marian Sang: The True Recital of Marian Anderson, Voice of a Century*. New York, NY: Scholastic.

Sheinkin, Steve. 2012. *Bomb: The Race to Build—and Steal—the World's Most Dangerous Weapon.* New York, NY: Roaring Brook Press.

Stier, Catherine. 2004. *If I Were President.* Park Ridge, IL: Albert Whitman & Company.

Van Allsburg, Chris. 2004. *The Mysteries of Harris Burdick*, The Portfolio Edition. Boston, MA: Houghton Mifflin.

Wilson, Vincent Jr. 2013. *The Book of the Presidents: With Portraits by Distinguished American Artists*. Brookeville, MD: American History Research Associates.

Yu, Chun. 2005. *Little Green: Growing up in the Chinese Cultural Revolution.* New York, NY: Simon & Schuster.

Websites

Reading and Literacy

Aaron Shepard's Reader's Theatre Page
http://www.aaronshep.com/rt/

The International Literacy Association
http://www.reading.org

Lesson Plans from The International Literacy Association
http://www.readwritethink.org

National Writing Project
http://www.nwp.org/

Pixton
http://www.pixton.com/

Reading Rockets
http://www.readingrockets.org

ReadWriteThink.org Comic Creator
http://www.readwritethink.org/files/resources/interactives/comic/cartoon10.swf

Starfall
http://www.starfall.com/

Math

Macmillan Children's
http://www.mackids.com

Math Olympiads for Elementary and Middle Schools
http://www.moems.org

National Council of Teachers of Mathematics
http://www.nctm.org

NCTM Illuminations
http://illuminations.nctm.org/

Science

Adler Planetarium and Astronomy Museum, Chicago, IL
http://www.adlerplanetarium.org/

The American Association for the Advancement of Science
http://www.aaas.org/

American Museum of Natural History, New York, NY
http://www.amnh.org

Geology.com Teaching Earth Science
http://www.geology.com/teacher/

Museum of Science, Boston, MA
http://www.mos.org/

National Academy of Sciences
http://www.nasonline.org/

National Aeronautics and Space Administration (NASA)
http://www.nasa.gov/

National Science Foundation
http://www.nsf.gov/

National Science Teachers Association
http://www.nsta.org/

National Wildlife Federation
http://www.nwf.org/

Terrific Science
http://terrificscience.org/

Workman Publishing
http://www.workman.com/familytree/

Social Studies

American Rhetoric: Online Speech Bank
http://www.americanrhetoric.com/speechbank.htm

College, Career, and Civic Life (C3) Framework for Social Studies State Standards
http://www.socialstudies.org/c3

Center for Civic Education
http://civiced.org/

Facing History and Ourselves
https://www.facinghistory.org/

National Council for Geographic Education
http://www.ncge.org/

National Council for the Social Studies
http://www.socialstudies.org/

National History Day
http://www.nhd.org/

Teaching Tolerance
http://www.tolerance.org/

Figure 4.2 Oral Presentation Feedback Guidelines

Presenter's Name _____

Responder's Name _____

Title or Topic of Presentation _____

Directions: Rate the presenter on a scale of 1–5; write the number of your rating to the right of the question.

5 = Excellent 4 = Very Good 3 = Good 2 = Fair 1 = Poor

Criteria	Excellent	Very Good	Good	Fair	Poor
There was a clear opening statement or introductory section that introduced the topic and main ideas and gave a brief overview of the whole presentation.					
The thesis or main overarching idea of the talk was presented clearly. What was it? _____ _____ _____					
The presentation was organized clearly in a logical sequence from start to finish. What were the main points? _____ _____ _____					
The main points or ideas were supported by sufficient facts, details, and evidence.					

Criteria	Excellent	Very Good	Good	Fair	Poor
The presenter used clear transitional words and phrases to move smoothly from one main point to the next. What are some examples of transitional words that this presenter used? _____ _____ _____					
There was a clear concluding section.					
The conclusion used some of the same words from the opening statement, thesis, or main idea. Or, the presenter decided to end with a new, thought-provoking question for the audience.					
The speaker maintained good eye contact with the audience.					
The speaker acted poised and used appropriate gestures occasionally for emphasis.					
The presenter spoke in a clear, audible voice that could be heard throughout the room.					
The speaker used appropriate language and clear pronunciation.					
If the speaker used visual aids, they were well-prepared, informative, effective, and not distracting.					
Comments: I liked _____ _____ To make future presentations even better, I suggest _____ _____					

Notes